The HEARTBEAT of GOD

The HEARTBEAT *of* GOD

Finding the Sacred in the Middle of Everything

KATHARINE JEFFERTS SCHORI

FOREWORD BY JOAN CHITTISTER, OSB

Walking Together, Finding the Way®
SKYLIGHT PATHS®
PUBLISHING
Woodstock, Vermont

The Heartbeat of God:
Finding the Sacred in the Middle of Everything

2011 Hardcover Edition, First Printing
© 2011 by Katharine Jefferts Schori
Foreword © 2011 by Joan Chittister

Library of Congress Cataloging-in-Publication Data
Jefferts Schori, Katharine.
The heartbeat of God : finding the sacred in the middle of everything / Katharine Jefferts Schori. — Hardcover ed.
  p. cm.
Includes bibliographical references.
ISBN 978-1-59473-292-8 (hardcover)
1. Spirituality. 2. Christian life. 3. Religious life. 4. Church and social problems. 5. Religion and sociology. I. Title. II. Title: Finding the sacred in the middle of everything.
BV4501.3.J43 2010
248—dc22

                                                                2010036777

10   9   8   7   6   5   4   3   2   1

Manufactured in the United States of America
Jacket Design: Jenny Buono

> SkyLight Paths Publishing is creating a place where people of different spiritual traditions come together for challenge and inspiration, a place where we can help each other understand the mystery that lies at the heart of our existence.
>
> SkyLight Paths sees both believers and seekers as a community that increasingly transcends traditional boundaries of religion and denomination—people wanting to learn from each other, *walking together, finding the way.*

Walking Together, Finding the Way®
Published by SkyLight Paths Publishing
A Division of Longhill Partners, Inc.
Sunset Farm Offices, Route 4, P.O. Box 237
Woodstock, VT 05091
Tel: (802) 457-4000   Fax: (802) 457-4004
www.skylightpaths.com

For Bruce and Barbara,
who have taught me much about the heart of God
in the midst of intimate community.

Contents

Foreword

Welcome to one of the most exciting books most of us have seen come out of a church for a long, long time—if ever. It is creative in its homiletics. It is current in its content. It is honest in its analyses. And it is brave in its selection of subject matter. More than that, it is by a bishop—a woman bishop! Those perspectives alone could put it in the category of "rare book" and "good theology."

It is, in other words, not the kind of writing we are accustomed to getting from officials of a church. Any church. There are no limp, lifeless clichés for what it means to be a Christian. There are no pat and hackneyed phrases meant to soften our Christian duty to look at what we're seeing and then deal with what we're looking at in both church and state.

More than that, there is no triumphalism in this book, meaning the tendency of churches to announce themselves in lieu of announcing the reign of God. There is no divinization of the institution itself. In fact, though there is a great deal of love, respect, and affection for the tradition that is Anglicanism and for the missionary history of U.S. Episcopalianism, this book is more about the application of the gospel to the challenges particular to these times than it is a paean to either system.

The book is fresh in its approach, deeply knowledgeable in its presentation of issues, and unrelentingly uncompromising in its realistic appraisal of the need for the church to be the word it preaches. This book does not excoriate its members for their personal sins. Instead, it warns the church itself about parading sinlessness as a substitute for the social justice the heart of God requires.

For that reason alone, *The Heartbeat of God* should be read, studied, and discussed in every parish hall of every Christian tradition, Episcopalian or not, so that the renewal of the church may finally, finally begin in a world that knows that the revolution that is Jesus is long overdue.

—JOAN CHITTISTER, OSB

Acknowledgments

I am deeply grateful for the creative work of my editor, Nancy Fitzgerald. Her drive and imagination have brought this book into being.

I have people to thank in all parts of The Episcopal Church, and across the globe in other parts of the Anglican Communion, for their deep and gracious hospitality to a sojourner in their midst. I have been privileged to see, learn about, and share in the transformative gospel work being done in many, many places. God's world is being healed, person by person, community by community, thanks to the vision of so many people of faith.

The work I do would not be possible without those who assist so ably in my office: Neva Rae Fox, Canon Chuck Robertson, Sharon Jones, Miguel Escobar, Ednice Baerga, and Linda Watt, who keeps all the work of The Episcopal Church Center running like a fine Swiss watch. The heart of mission beats strongly among all who serve the wider Episcopal Church, and their work continues to inspire me.

Introduction

I went running in the dark this morning. There were people sleeping under almost every overpass—dark bundles turned away from the path, yet still in view in the scattered streetlights, seeking a fragment of safety. When somebody asks them Jesus' question—"What do you want me to do for you?"—their answer is often: "Pray with me."

I think that's the same answer most of us would give: Help me see hope in the midst of my pain, celebrate with me when I rejoice, let me know I'm not alone. Those folks asleep under the bridges have names, too, names that start with "beloved" and "pleasing to God." It's up to us to learn their names and call them friend. This road we are all on is no place for strangers.

In the aftermath of the recent economic crisis, in the face of the Gulf oil spill, in the midst of continuing concerns over immigration, the Christian tradition continues to insist that the well-being of all members of society is the necessary focus and concern of each member of it. When the poorest members are further marginalized and victimized, society as a whole has a responsibility both to care for those on the edges and to continually work to shift social structures toward greater justice.

This ethic of care for the least among us applies to all the major issues facing us everywhere: local, national, and international economic practices; ecological and climatic concerns; and the structure of the global market. The burdens of both inaction and change cannot be assigned to the poorest members of society without ultimately destroying our society. Kids whose families lack health insurance, for instance, miss more school days, get lower grades, eventually earn lower wages—and are less likely to be productive workers when they grow up.[1] Financial shenanigans on Wall Street lead to unemployment on Main Street. Doing nothing hurts everyone. We're all in this together.

While the economic destruction of the past few years has in some ways begun to moderate, the immediate benefits appear to be flowing to the wealthiest—money managers, bankers, and investors. But those whose jobs and livelihoods have been lost have suffered much greater setbacks and have yet to experience any substantial recovery. A more just societal structure would slow the economic advantaging of the wealthiest so that the poorest might sooner reach at least a minimal standard of living.

Environmental concerns are often the focus of energetic discussion by more privileged members of society, even though the negative impacts usually fall more heavily on the poorest. The inequitable effects of industrial pollution are well known, though often ignored. Poorer governments—and sometimes even poorer neighborhoods—tolerate levels of environmental destruction and contamination, in the "interests" of economic development, which would be considered anathema in wealthier places. So the poor are multiply impacted—at the least through more sickness and shorter life spans, and sometimes through reduced cognitive capacity and educational advancement, the frequent result of heavy metals pollution. Those poorer countries and cities and neighborhoods are also amassing a long-term environmental burden far greater than any short-term economic benefit. Such practices deprive the poor of any realistic ability to develop in sustainable ways.

Without major efforts by wealthier communities, the global effects of climate change will be borne most heavily by those least able to respond. The low-lying areas of the South Pacific and coasts of south Asia are already being affected by rising sea level, flooding, and storm surges. In the United States, the experience of a flooded New Orleans following Hurricane Katrina in 2005 is a very small but powerful example of what is looming. Food production in already marginal areas—such as much of sub-Saharan Africa—will become more and more difficult as rainfall patterns shift and the land becomes less productive. Worsening shortages of water will only continue in the western United States. Ensuing migration in search of food, water, and grazing will only increase conflict between those with few or no resources and those with more.

All these issues are exacerbated by corruption in both wealthy and poorer nations, as aid from well-meaning rich nations is siphoned into the pockets of already-wealthy nationals in developing areas, and as finances are mismanaged even in our own country.

An ethic of shared sacrifice or investment by the better-off will be increasingly important as we face these global issues and their consequences. If the wealthy of this world continue to reap out-sized profits in the face of mounting poverty, then violence and bloodshed, and ensuing global insecurity, can be the only expected result. Even a narrow self-interest must begin to work on a longer time scale and a larger geographic one. Including longer-term environmental costs in basic economic calculations is one way of doing so.

We are all connected—as human beings with one another, as Americans with other Americans, as one nation with all others, and as the human species with the whole of our environment. The behavior of each has consequences for all. Our decision making must consider the welfare of those others in addition to our own, for they are intimately connected. With a world population of seven billion we can no longer—if indeed we ever could—afford to ignore those interconnections. The welfare of the least among us and around us will eventually be our own.

As Christians—indeed as people of faith of any tradition—we are called to tend to the needs of these least among us. Our response to them must be the response of faith. God gives us a new heart to do this work, and every time we gather to do it, God offers a pacemaker jolt to tweak our heart's rhythm. The challenge is this: Will our hearts respond with a strengthened beat, in tune with God's own heartbeat, sending more life out into the world?

We are all running down the same road, and our task is to break through the obstacles and make the road smoother for one another. If you read the Hebrew Scriptures closely, you discover that God's promise of full larders and planted fields and repopulated cities is followed by *metanoia*—a new mind and a new heart.

So, how will this heart push more lifeblood out into a languishing world? This book will look at the many ways our faith and our lives intersect—and how we can respond to this heartbeat of God.

Can you hear the beat?

Part One

Connecting with the Margins

For I was hungry and you gave me something to eat, I was thirsty and you gave me something to drink, I was a stranger and you welcomed me.

—MATTHEW 25:35

As Christians, caring for the poor and the sick is our gospel mandate. Jesus began his ministry in his hometown synagogue, announcing that he'd come to bring good news to the poor and oppressed, and he spent the rest of his life tending to their needs. Indeed, he was following a long and noble tradition that went back to the earliest days of the Hebrew people. "If there is a poor man among your brothers in any of the towns of the land that the Lord your God is giving you," wrote the author of the book of Deuteronomy, "do not be hard-hearted or tight-fisted toward your poor brother" (Deuteronomy 15:7; NIV). The chapters that follow will take a look at our fundamental connection with the poor and the sick that offers us the chance not only to share our own abundance and bring Jesus' healing touch, but also to receive the blessing that they offer us.

Serving the Poor

What does the Lord require of you but to do justice, and to love mercy, and to walk humbly with your God?

—MICAH 6:8 (my translation)

Let justice roll down like waters, and righteousness like an ever-flowing stream.

—AMOS 5:24

The Spirit of the Lord is upon me, because he has anointed me to bring good news to the poor. He has sent me to proclaim release to the captives and recovery of sight to the blind, to let the oppressed go free, to proclaim the year of the Lord's favor.

—LUKE 4:18–19

This is the meaning of life, in twenty-five words or less: We're here to do justice and love mercy, to walk humbly with God and bring good news to the poor. We're here to proclaim the ancient visions of the commonweal of God, where everyone has enough to eat and no one goes thirsty or homeless; where all have access to meaningful employment and health care; where the wealthy and powerful do not exploit the weak; and where no one studies war any more. We're here to bring the good news of justice, which includes the work of building community and caring for the earth, which are essential to the health of a spiritually rooted person, in right relationship with God and neighbor.

3

The Episcopal Church, with its partners both sacred and secular, is part of that mission of God's to bring that holy dream to reality. Though the principles apply beyond these shores, let's focus here on building that reality within these United States. How can all the people of this nation participate in the abundance that is already here?

ENDING HUNGER

If your enemies are hungry, give them bread to eat; and if they are thirsty, give them water to drink.

—PROVERBS 25:21

First things come first. Before we do anything else, we must feed the hungry. God's vision of abundance is holistic—it's about the well-being of the whole person and the whole community—and it begins with a feast. Thousands of years ago, the prophets of the Hebrew Scriptures dreamed about it: "On this mountain the Lord of hosts will make for all peoples a feast of rich food, a feast of well-aged wines, of rich food filled with marrow, of well-aged wines strained clear. And he will destroy on this mountain the shroud that is cast over all peoples, the sheet that is spread over all nations. He will swallow up death forever" (Isaiah 25:6–8). For some reason we hear this passage most often at funerals, as though the feast is too utopian for this life. Well, Jesus didn't think so—he made a habit of feasting, so much so that some people called him a party animal.

But here in America, in a nation that is one of the largest producers and exporters of food in the world, far too many people struggle to find sufficient food every day, from Native Americans whose local grocery store only sells chips and soda to those who live in the food deserts of our inner cities, where the well-stocked supermarkets that suburbanites take for granted simply do not exist. Many of our critically important efforts to respond to this food problem simply try to provide enough calories—almost anything to stave off starvation. But what's really needed is not just calories but also a nutritious and adequate diet for people of all ages, from pregnant mothers to children and elders. None will be healthy, none will know the fullness of God's intent for each one of us until daily bread is within the reach of every person—daily protein, vegetables, and fruit, too, and enough extra for a feast.

Nutrition is the base of the pyramid of well-being. When each person has an adequate diet, most of the rest of God's dream of commonweal will have been achieved. One of the real tragedies of poverty is that there are so many tradeoffs that involve choices between food and medicine, food and shelter, decent food and transportation to a job.

The irony isn't just that we have more than enough decent food to feed everyone in this nation an adequate diet, but that so many of us have such an unhealthy relationship with food. Lots of Americans have too much to eat, and the epidemic of illness related to overconsumption is a sign of rampant spiritual dis-ease. The work of alleviating physical hunger must be addressed to all of us, and by all of us, beginning with attention to how, why, and what we eat. If our congregations, or communities, or organizations want to work on hunger, we can start by looking at our own relationships to food. Here's an example: An ecumenical effort in Oregon a couple of years ago invited people to live on a food stamp budget for a week. The governor's family made it a public exercise.

If we want to move beyond simply doling out calories to the hungry, there's a menu of significant options. Nutrition education—classes that teach how to plan, shop for, and cook healthy meals on a budget—and local gardens are possibilities. They are also ways to break down some of the barriers between the hungry and the well fed. Consider how much farther our collective food dollars would stretch if we encouraged everyone in our communities to eat a greater proportion of seasonal local produce rather than foods that require long-distance transportation, such as imported fish, fruit, and vegetables, or foods that are highly resource-intensive, such as most commercially raised meat.

I've been astounded at the number of schools I've seen recently that are planting gardens, from a child-care center in Bridgeport, Connecticut, where each kid is planting two favorite vegetables in a milk crate, to a rooftop greenhouse in New York City that produces salad and veggies for the school cafeteria. Almost every church I've ever seen has some green space, some of which could be used to grow food. Why do we mow great expanses of lawn in the suburbs rather than farm carrots or tend peaches? There's a church in Smyrna, Tennessee, that had twenty acres of rich bottomland that parishioners had been planning to turn into a softball field until a group of Burmese Anglican immigrants turned up and asked if they could come there to worship. It quickly became evident that these refugees were almost all out-of-work farmers. There is now an expanding truck garden on that fertile land, producing large crops of fine Asian vegetables, most of which are contracted for before they're even planted. Food and the dignity of being able to support a family go together.

Even churches in dense urban environments, surrounded by asphalt and concrete, can have powerful feeding ministries. Some of them are soup kitchens—and it doesn't appear that the need for basic calories is going away any time soon. Some of the more creative ones expand the menu to include other kinds of ministry, such as the writing group at Holy Apostles Church in New York City, or the art program at Welcome Table in the District of Columbia. Some congregations even offer bulk shopping as a way to increase food choices and reduce costs for those without private transportation. Some churches provide space for farmers' markets or contract with a local grower to provide baskets of seasonal produce. Adding fresh produce to a sack of staple groceries can significantly improve the quality of food-pantry calories. A church in Queens, New York, partners with Harvest Astoria, a community-supported agriculture group upstate to bring affordable, fresh, nutritious food to city-dwellers and to promote an ongoing conversation about what we eat and how it affects our bodies, communities, and environment.

Geneticists are beginning to understand that it's not just the total caloric input that's essential to ongoing health, and that the impact of diet extends to new generations. The quality of a pregnant woman's diet has significant effects on her child's later health, including susceptibility to obesity, diabetes, and cancer—and those effects may extend to her grandchildren as well. Studies show measurable third-generation effects as a result of famine in the Netherlands at the end of World War II.[1]

We have long suspected such effects as a result of poverty on reservations and in the inner city. That old proverb about the parents eating sour grapes and the children's teeth being set on edge (Jeremiah 31:29) may have implications we never imagined.

FINDING WATER

> *Then the king will say to those at his right hand, "Come, you that are blessed by my Father, inherit the kingdom prepared for you from the foundation of the world; for I was hungry and you gave me food, I was thirsty and you gave me something to drink."*
> —MATTHEW 25:34–35

Access to clean water is one of the benchmarks of the Millennium Development Goals, the United Nations initiatives that seek to improve conditions for the poorest of the poor in developing nations. But it is also of growing significance here, within the United States. Although most communities have access to clean drinking water, a number of towns and cities deal with the legacy of environmental pollution, and the poor are almost everywhere disproportionately affected. There are significant poor populations within the United States who simply do not have access to basic water and sanitation:

the homeless, migrant farm workers, parts of several Indian reservations, and some isolated rural households. Every summer, people die in the deserts of the Southwest for lack of access to drinking water, clean or not. Most of them are either homeless or migrating. Many more, across the country, suffer from inadequate sanitation and lack of sufficient clean water. This is a little-noticed problem, but in some places it can be as significant as it is in some third-world nations.

The larger issues of water and poverty in the United States have to do with overextraction of water from aquifers and with the environmental consequences of climate change. As the planet continues to warm, we will see increased drought, shifting crop production, and changes in the ability to grow traditional crops in various geographic areas. The poor will most assuredly be disproportionately affected, and least able to respond. For example, the rural poor who depend on wells for both domestic and agricultural water will be less able to respond to depleting aquifers than large-scale commercial agriculture will be.

The aftermath of Hurricane Katrina—both the immediate need in the midst of crisis to provide drinking water and sanitation, and the longer-term response of restoring municipal waterworks—is a sad example of how poverty is related to water availability in denser urban areas. Water issues are little noticed in much of the poverty work that churches and other organizations do, but they need attention in many localities. Domestic water policy and mission work could benefit by learning from and partnering with international water organizations. There are a number of U.S. government programs that focus on water issues, but the work they do is rarely linked directly to underlying problems of poverty.

ENDING HOMELESSNESS

> *And Jesus said to him, "Foxes have holes, and birds of the air have nests; but the Son of Man has nowhere to lay his head."*
> —MATTHEW 8:20

It may have been fine for Jesus to live out of a suitcase, but most of us are meant to have homes to live in. Our most distinctive image of poverty in this country has to do with whether or not a person has a home. Once we passed the immediate crisis of Katrina, building and rebuilding homes for the displaced became a central focus. The Episcopal Church, along with other communities of faith, continues to address poverty in New Orleans and on the Mississippi coast, as well as throughout the country, through seeking to shelter those without adequate homes.

Much of the impact of the recent fiscal crisis on the poorer segments of our society has been felt in the loss of home value and foreclosure. Housing stability has been lost for countless thousands of individuals and families. Our response as a church has been varied: continuing work with programs such as Habitat for Humanity that seek to provide individual home ownership through volunteer labor and donated materials; opening and expanding shelter facilities for temporary housing; providing transitional housing, including programs such as Family Promise, which facilitates moves to more permanent housing arrangements; and constructing low- and mixed-income housing. St. Paul's Development Corporation in Savannah, Georgia, is an example of how a congregation can transform an entire neighborhood through working to provide affordable housing. Every congregation, every faith community, no matter its size, can partner in some way to provide shelter and housing for one or more people.

It's appropriate to consider ministries that address clothing needs as well—from providing winter coats and hats to schoolchildren and the homeless, to offering business clothing to those seeking new employment. In the Hebrew Scriptures, the covenant laws focusing on justice for the poor centered on debts and pledges, and forbid onerous and unjust collections by a lender from a debtor: "If you take your neighbor's cloak in pawn, you shall restore it before the sun goes down; for it may be your neighbor's only clothing to use as cover; in what else shall that person sleep?" (Exodus 22:26–27). A poor person who offered his cloak in pledge against a debt would need that garment as his evening shelter, so it could not justly be held overnight.

Each of these ministries addresses different aspects of the need for shelter. Some of them, such as shelter beds, are examples of crisis intervention and some, such as transitional housing and Habitat for Humanity, are longer-term solutions. But rarely do these ministries address the structural issues that result in homelessness. It's not until we get to intentional work that mixes economic classes or advocates for different solutions that we get to the heart of the matter. In the same way that congregational study about food and nutrition might cut across economic divides, so too is intentional boundary crossing needed in regard to housing. Most of our towns and cities are still highly segregated economically, and both civic amenities and infra-structure usually reflect the difference, privileging the wealthy. Schools are of varying quality, the kind and availability of grocery stores reflect the neighborhood's poverty or affluence, and industrial zoning rarely impacts wealthier sections of town. Justice, though, expects that all have access to the abundance for which we were cre-ated, and that none of us enjoys radical excess while some are in want.

DEALING WITH MONEY

> *If you lend money to my people, to the poor among you, you shall not deal with them as a creditor; you shall not exact interest from them.*
>
> —EXODUS 22:25

The current economic ills of this nation—indeed, of the globe—are largely the result of greed and the unwillingness of govern-ments to limit profits. They are largely the result of usury. The Hebrew Scriptures prohibit taking interest from fellow members of the religious community, and collecting interest is what *usury* originally meant. There were some permissible exceptions—

profit from the use of money was acceptable if the risk was shared between lender and receiver, and interest could be charged to those outside the religious community. The church carried this prohibition into developing Christianity, and for centuries Jewish moneylenders were essentially the only source of credit in Christian communities in Europe. We rarely talk about the financial aspects of anti-Semitism, but this history is a contributing part. Significant change came in England under Henry VIII in 1545, in an act that permitted anyone to charge up to 10 percent interest on loaned money. We've been paying an increasing price ever since.

In the United States today, usury is defined by state statute, with little national regulation. Banks and other financial institutions largely avoid local usury statutes through specific legal exemptions or by establishing their headquarters in a state with weak restrictions. The result in recent years has been exorbitant credit card rates and predatory lending practices. Usury, particularly in the sense of excessive and exorbitant profit, is rampant. The poor are being exploited all around us, and excessive interest rates contribute mightily to keeping people locked in poverty. Growing awareness and critique of such practices has produced initiatives that seek to limit interest to 10 percent, though such a move will undoubtedly be politically very difficult to enact.

Many approaches are possible, beyond legal reform. Financial education for all would be an excellent beginning strategy. This education needs to include all, not just the poor, in the context of stewardship of the gifts God has given, and it needs to encourage all of us to think deeply about the financial decisions we make. When is contracting debt a reasonable decision? How do faithful people manage their money—what kinds of information, approaches, and decisions are important? Learning about the interconnected global economic system is a significant aspect of Christian stewardship, and should inform our civic duties as well.

Educated congregations and larger faith organizations can engage proactively by establishing credit unions and micro-lending opportunities—both can be effective ways of liberating people from predatory practices. Such initiatives also present creative ecumenical and interfaith possibilities, using the gifts already present in a community to respond to local need.

We have an important but little-known resource in The Episcopal Church's Economic Justice Loan Fund. Some seven million dollars are available, in a revolving loan fund, for development partnerships in communities that lack sufficient access to financial capital. The funds can be used for economic development, social services, and job creation. The loans are not made to end users, but to local community financial institutions—and can be an important encouragement to the establishment of loan funds, credit unions, and other local economic development initiatives. To support economic redevelopment in the aftermath of Hurricane Katrina, for instance, the Loan Fund deposited one hundred thousand dollars with credit unions in Louisiana and Mississippi.

Meaningful and adequate employment opportunities are an essential part of addressing the worst of domestic poverty. The unemployment rate on Native American reservations is often 50 to 80 percent, and in inner cities up to 40 or 50 percent of young black males are often without jobs. These are deeply systemic issues, reflecting a major shift in our economic engine, as well as inadequate education and job training, economic investment, and job creation. The challenges of employment are exacerbated by insufficient affordable child care, which offers another poverty-alleviation strategy available to many local congregations.

I recently had a conversation with some homeless men—some of whom held jobs—in Washington, D.C. One man told me that economic studies show that a living wage in the District would need to be $24 per hour, based on average housing costs of about $1,400 a month.[2] The Bureau of Labor Statistics said that was too high, and set it at $12.50 an hour.[3]

How many congregations and other faith communities are leading ministries that focus on full employment? Or entrepreneurial laboratories that help to match people's skills and talents with employment possibilities? They are out there—many feeding programs expand into case management, shelter, and employment assistance. St. Stephen's Episcopal Church in Grand Island, Nebraska, subsidizes a one-stop community ministry coalition in a building adjacent to the church, offering food, shelter, and literacy and education ministries, as well as Habitat for Humanity and the United Way. The Diocese of Los Angeles runs a culinary training program called Mama's Kitchen, which grew out of its support for artisanal food vendors (Mama's Hot Tamales).

EDUCATING OUR YOUTH

> But Jesus called for them and said, "Let the little children come to me, and do not stop them; for it is to such as these that the kingdom of God belongs."
>
> —LUKE 18:16

In addition to hunger, the most ancient and traditional service ministries of The Episcopal Church have been focused on healing and education, reflecting Jesus' own ministry of feeding, healing, and teaching. Schools continue to be an essential part of our ministry—they help transform lives and they are central to addressing poverty. Two schools in the greater Boston area, Esperanza Academy and Epiphany, both work with poor inner-city middle-school students and their families, equipping them to succeed in competitive secondary and higher education. They do remarkable work. Bishop Walker School in Washington, D.C., is focused on at-risk boys and their families in a poor section of the city. St.

Mark's Day Care in Bridgeport, Connecticut, works with pre-school and kindergarten children, and facilitates after-school enrichment for students through middle school. St. James Family Center in Cathlamet, Washington, serves children and families through preschool, Head Start, parenting classes, teen programs, and community programs that foster education and healthy development.

The best education focuses on the whole person—with attention to physical, intellectual, emotional, spiritual, and cultural growth and enrichment. The Diocese of Mississippi is engaged in important conversations about how The Episcopal Church can most appropriately serve the range of educational needs in their communities, and not limit the church's educational mission to the wealthy or those who are academically competitive. That is an important discussion everywhere, and it is connected to our understanding that all God's children have gifts for ministry, that all people have a role in the transformation of this society toward something that looks more like the reign of God.

These successful schools include families because they understand that education focused on families and communities together can have a far greater impact on poverty than education that's focused solely on individuals. We are all interconnected. One of the clearest predictors of a child's success in life is the presence of interested and unrelated adults—mentors, coaches, grandparents, and *padrinos y madrinas* (godparents). When a community is invested in children's success, everyone comes closer to abundant life.

SEEKING CULTURAL AND STRUCTURAL JUSTICE

> *You shall not render an unjust judgment; you shall not be partial to the poor or defer to the great: with justice you shall judge your neighbor.*
>
> —LEVITICUS 19:15

All of these issues—food and water, debt, employment, and education—lead us to the larger systemic issues of poverty, and the particular challenges of Native American reservations and inner-city minority communities. Both exist in the midst of a dominant culture that has worked hard, both unintentionally and by conscious policy, to eliminate those cultural differences. Native Americans, as well as African Americans and many other ethnic groups, have been the subject of cultural "cleansing." Poverty also has something to do with cultural injustice and racism.

The determination of The Episcopal Church's triennial General Convention in the summer of 2009 to address domestic poverty included a strategic decision to focus initially on First Nations peoples, or Native Americans. We hope that the strategic responses that emerge from this initiative will provide models, examples, and success stories that can be applied in other communities.

Poor Native American communities often experience levels of violence far higher than those found in dominant culture environments, particularly exceedingly high suicide rates among young people. On some reservations, the suicide rate is ten times what it is in America generally. Violent behavior in general spikes in communities where poverty is rampant, and hopelessness has something to do with it. Restoring dignity in the midst of environments where traditional cultures have been denied can have positive impacts on the interrelated system of violence and poverty.

Equipping leaders to make and own decisions, strategies, and priorities is essential to development and the relief of poverty. We're learning how to do this—and it has much to do with affirming the gifts that are already present. Asset-Based Community Development (ABCD) is one framework for this kind of endeavor. ABCD is an approach that focuses on uncovering the strengths that communities already have—the skills of the residents and the resources of local organizations such as churches, neighborhood groups, and schools—and helps them harness those strengths to build a better community.

Discerning gifts for ministry—prayerfully considering the talents God has given us and figuring out how to use them to serve others—is another. There is a very natural and appropriate connection between the two. The work of White Bison, a program that offers sobriety, recovery, addiction prevention, and wellness resources to Native American communities, is about this kind of dignity and self-determination.

WORKING FOR HEALING, HEALTH, AND WHOLENESS

> *Jesus went throughout Galilee, teaching in their synagogues and proclaiming the good news of the kingdom and curing every disease and every sickness among the people.*
>
> —MATTHEW 4:23

Cultural healing and restoring dignity may focus on the healing of communities, yet they are likely to have more prosaic health benefits as well. Addressing the physical and mental health of individuals is also a major aspect of addressing poverty.

The poor have far higher rates of preventable disease and chronic illness, often as a result of structural injustice—the lack of adequate food, clean water, and predictable shelter and employment, as well as access to preventive and other forms of health care. The very stresses of living in poverty contribute to many forms of disease. Aspects of the genome actually change in response to that kind of stress, permitting or preventing the expression of genes related to disease prevention and immune response.

As communities of faith, we can address these realities in a variety of ways—through health screenings, parish nursing programs, and medical clinics, ensuring access to addiction treatment and mental health resources, as well as the kind of advocacy work with governments that is required to transform the structures of injustice.

This is all the kind of reconciliation work that is mandated by Jesus when he told his apostles "to love one another as I have loved you" (John 13:34; my translation).

Peacemaking on the local and global level will release enormous resources to address issues of poverty. Peacemaking that is concerned for people and the planet will help heal deep poverty. We've already looked at the ways that the fear and anxiety that come with living in violent environments impact basic health, but the structural aspects of resource expenditure on war divert resources from basic human needs. Providing basic health care for everyone in this country would be a relatively trivial issue economically if our defense budget went on a diet.

DEALING WITH CLIMATE CHANGE AND THE ENVIRONMENT

> God saw everything that he had made, and indeed, it was very good.
>
> —GENESIS 1:31

Healing the worst of the poverty in this nation is intrinsically connected to restoring human beings to right relationship with creation. Global climate change will have its most devastating effects on the poorest, who are least able to respond and adapt. The educational efforts we can undertake in congregations can provide an important impetus toward solidarity with the poor. How willing are the wealthier among us to limit our consumption patterns and change our lifestyles so that all people might have the necessities of life? A relatively minor alteration in carbon use for fuel and power—in driving less, recycling water, or washing dishes rather than using expanded foam products—if spread across large populations, will permit others to improve their standard of living. It's basically an issue of selfishness versus sharing.

CREATING A NEW HEAVEN AND A NEW EARTH

*Then I saw a new heaven and a new earth; for the first heaven and
the first earth had passed away, and the sea was no more. And I
saw the holy city, the new Jerusalem, coming down out of heaven
from God, prepared as a bride adorned for her husband. And
I heard a loud voice from the throne saying, "See, the home of
God is among mortals. He will dwell with them; they will be his
peoples, and God himself will be with them."*

—REVELATION 21:1–3

Whenever we recite the Lord's Prayer, we pray that God's kingdom
will come, and that we will have daily bread. That vision of the reign
of God is about adequate food, water, shelter, the resources that
come from employment and education, healing, and communities
that live in right relationship with God and neighbor—both human
and the rest of creation. Sometimes this vision of God's peaceful
reign is called *shalom*—more than an absence of war, *shalom* brings an
end to all violence and is an essential part of the abundant life for
which Jesus came among us.

How can we work together to move more effectively toward
that holy dream? Our task is to dream that dream, and look for
strategies, partnerships, collaborations, networking, and the gifts
that God has already given us to make that dream a reality. Our task
is to discover how we can claim those words of Jesus for our own—
to bring good news to the poor, release to the captives, sight to the
blind, freedom to the oppressed. Our mission is the mission of
Jesus—and our job is to be able to say, as he did, "Today, this scripture is being fulfilled in our hearing" (Luke 4:21; my translation).

For Reflection

What are some ways we can live more simply so that others may simply live? Where do we see the connection between our well-being and the well-being of others?

Healing for All

A leper came to him begging him, and kneeling he said to him, "If you choose, you can make me clean." Moved with pity, Jesus stretched out his hand and touched him, and said to him, "I do choose. Be made clean!" Immediately the leprosy left him, and he was made clean. After sternly warning him he sent him away at once, saying to him, "See that you say nothing to anyone; but go, show yourself to the priest, and offer for your cleansing what Moses commanded, as a testimony to them." But he went out and began to proclaim it freely, and to spread the word, so that Jesus could no longer go into a town openly, but stayed out in the country; and people came to him from every quarter.

—MARK 1:40–45

AIDS has often been likened to a modern-day leprosy. When it emerged as a global pandemic, it produced the same kind of horror, misunderstanding, and discrimination that leprosy did in the ancient world. The disease that's identified as leprosy in the Bible is probably several different skin conditions, Hansen's disease among them. But the social isolation was the same for all, and it's the same for people with AIDS today.

There are many parallels between leprosy and AIDS. Hansen's disease was the first human disease to be identified with a particular microorganism, in 1873. AIDS was first described about a hundred years later, in 1981, and very quickly identified with the Human

Immunodeficiency Virus. But an understanding of the disease process, and effective treatments for each of them, took a long time. Hansen's disease, to which only a small portion of human beings are susceptible, is far less threatening than is AIDS, which is much larger in scope—without treatment, about 90 percent of human beings infected with HIV progress to full-blown AIDS. Treatment for each disease consists of a lengthy course of several drugs, and while Hansen's disease can be largely arrested and contagiousness ended soon after treatment begins, we have not yet figured out how to end or cure an HIV infection.

The other and perhaps greater parallel between the two diseases is their social stigma. Lepers are described in ancient texts going back to at least the sixth century BCE, in the Bible, and in Chinese and Indian texts. Those with visible disease have often been segregated to live in different communities, excluded from normal social interactions. People known to be infected with HIV still lose jobs, family and friends, and normal social support in many parts of the world, including here in the United States.

The religious community has been among the first responders in both disease systems.

There are two healing stories in the Bible that have something significant to say about how people of faith respond not only to HIV/AIDS but also to any human condition that stigmatizes. In the Hebrew Scriptures, Naaman's story is a heart-breaker—and a heart-changer. A successful military leader, he is struck down by a disfiguring disease that's likely to get him ousted from his post in a society even more fixated on appearance than ours is. If Naaman can't get his skin cleaned up, not only will he have to leave office but he'll also be banished from polite and religiously observant society.

Naaman's route to healing reads almost like a spy novel. The Hebrew slave girl who works for his wife offers a shred of hope: there's a prophet in Israel, she says, who can cure Naaman of his disease. Her tiny thread of hope sends him rushing off to his king to get

a letter of passage to his enemy, the king of Israel, requesting healing. But when the Israeli king reads the letter, he despairs—he
knows that healing lepers is way outside his domain. The prophet
Elisha, though, gets wind of the story and sends word to the visitor:
"Come see me and I'll see what I can do." Naaman goes to Elisha's
house, where the prophet sends a message out to him, directing him
to "go wash in the Jordan, and you'll get what you're after."

Those orders sounded amazingly dismissive to Naaman, who
leaves in a huff. But his own servants convince him to take a dip in
the river anyway—what does he have to lose?—and he gets his
youthful appearance back. Slave girl, servants, enemies, kings, and
prophets—an impressive set of links that bring Naaman to his knees
(2 Kings 5).

The Christian gospel story of Jesus healing the leper is more
direct. In Mark 1:40–45, the leper presents himself to Jesus and asks to
be healed. Actually, he's a bit whiny about it: "If you really wanted to,"
he tells Jesus, "you could make me well." The English translation says
that Jesus was moved with pity, but the original Greek is a lot more
graphic. Jesus, it reads, "was moved in his guts." That means to feel
compassion—today we'd probably say that Jesus was "gut-wrenched."

Jesus reaches out his hand then, touches the leper, and says, "I *do*
want to; be clean." With this touch, Jesus chooses to foul himself, for
in the ancient world, touching a leper makes a person unfit for polite
society. But gut-wrenched, filled with compassion, Jesus touches the
man anyway, in spite of his own revulsion and the revulsion of the
people around him. Those onlookers, after all, just like the people
around Naaman, are accustomed to keeping themselves "clean" by
excluding anybody who threatens them. They don't want to get too
close, and they certainly don't want Jesus, their eminent visitor and
rabbi, to get too close, either.

But healing takes a whole community of unlikely partners, and it
takes getting past our own fear of contamination. Dealing with
AIDS in Madagascar or Miami takes an unlikely partnership of faith

communities and government agencies. Each group has its limits, but together a whole lot more healing goes on than if they went about their work separately. In order to heal, we too have to get beyond our understandings of who is clean and who is not. People of faith can work with other religious groups whose theologies they object to, and with environmentalists and atheists, if each of us is concerned about healing the pain and illness in the world around us.

The fear and stigma of illness has to be openly confronted and acknowledged. Most of Jesus' healings are from diseases such as leprosy and severe mental illness, which can't be hidden. You can hide your HIV status for a while, and many people do, because the reaction can be so intense. But check the gospels: Jesus doesn't heal anybody until he's asked.

Healing cannot begin until the one who is ill accepts the diagnosis. That's often the biggest hurdle, especially when the disease carries a stigma, such as addiction to alcohol or other drugs. In a twelve-step program, recovery only begins with acknowledgment of the addiction and the person's affirmation of powerlessness over it.

In a culture like ours that is so often addicted to other things such as shopping, or jockeying for position, or winning, it's not always easy to recognize or acknowledge what our illness really is. But that recognition is always essential to healing.

Even more than by the disease of leprosy, Jesus seems to be gut-wrenched by the leper's idea that this rabbi might choose *not* to heal him. Are we as energetically revolted by the idea that some people don't deserve to be healed? *That* idea really is what lies behind an unwillingness to heal our society. It is what made this nation so blind to the continuing crime of Katrina and its aftermath. It made us slow to respond to the genocide in Rwanda in the 1990s, and the AIDS epidemic here and around the world. The sense that some are more deserving than others has led us to wink at torture—"Well, it's OK if it's terrorists." It may have made us blind to the need for health-care reform in our country. But God won't let us off that hook.

God will use the children among us, and the people on the margins—servants, enemies, secularists, the poor, the stigmatized—to remind us that everybody can be healed, even the people we love to hate. God's mission is the healing of the whole world, and of every part of creation. That is the reason for Jesus' presence among us in human flesh. And it is the reason why each of us is here—to be healing hands and hearts and tongues.

For Reflection

Where will you start healing, and what will you continue to do to bring about healing in your life and your community? Who and what needs healing in your life and in your world?

Listening for the Voice of God

The Lord called Samuel again, a third time. And he got up and went to Eli, and said, "Here I am, for you called me." Then Eli perceived that the Lord was calling the boy. Therefore Eli said to Samuel, "Go, lie down; and if he calls you, you shall say, 'Speak, Lord, for your servant is listening.'" So Samuel went and lay down in his place.

—1 SAMUEL 3:8–9

The economic downturn that began a few years ago has affected everyone—even churches have not been immune from the financial woes that have afflicted this nation. The Episcopal Church Center in New York experienced major budget cuts, bringing grief and pain as staff departed and programs were ended or have begun to be done in radically different ways.

But in the wake of those changes, we also found enormous grace and energy as we gathered to look toward the future. It was a time of deep listening—both to the yearning of the church as a whole and to the immensely faithful will of the remaining staff to work together in new and creative ways.

That work is about the kind of listening that challenges Eli, a priest in the temple in Jerusalem, and Samuel, a young boy whom God has chosen to be a prophet. Samuel is awakened by a voice calling him in the middle of the night. Puzzled, he turns to Eli—but Eli doesn't get it either.

None of us understands in isolation—we need the larger community to help us discern not just the voice of God but also what that voice is saying. We need to stay in relationship, to build the kind of discerning community that will more readily hear the leading of the spirit even in the midst of life's challenges. The author of 1 Samuel, the book of Hebrew Scripture in which the story of Eli and the young Samuel appears, says that the word of the Lord was rare in those days and visions infrequent (1 Samuel 3:1). I'm not sure that the word of the Lord and spirited visions are any more common today than they were in the eleventh century BCE—but to those who attend, who wait on God, and listen with every fiber of their being, even with sleepy ears in the middle of the night, those calls and visions do come.

But how ready are we all to listen to one another? If God hears the cries of wanderers in the wilderness, that might be a good place to start. The hungry and hurting world around us is desperate for a word of good news. That's where Jesus started—good news to the poor, healing to the sick, the word of God to those who sought to learn—and all of it filled with compassion.

That work, that ministry, needs us all. The letter to the Ephesians in the Christian Scriptures starts by naming the ministries that the church has often reserved for the ordained: apostles, prophets, evangelists, pastors, even teachers—but none of those is solely the bailiwick of deacons or priests or bishops. All people of faith have a share in ministry. It's the last role in the list—the teacher—that is perhaps most important, because it equips new believers for ministry. That's how the labor is multiplied thirty-fold and sixty-fold and a hundredfold, resulting in a bountiful harvest.

Alda Marsh Morgan, a professor at the Church Divinity School of the Pacific in California, gave an interview in the August 24, 2009, issue of *Episcopal Life Online* about the effects of ordaining women, and she spoke with some pathos about one of the results being the devaluing of educated laywomen's vocations in the church. The Episcopal Church in the western United States was often planted and nurtured by deaconesses and single women missionaries, and later on, by Church Army workers who started Sunday schools, taught Native American children, nursed the sick, and raised the funds to build churches.

Dr. Morgan's lament is accurate, and it points to the reality that as a church, we really stopped listening in one very important respect. Dr. Morgan is herself profoundly deaf, but she has heard the cry of those whose ministries have been ignored. She has spoken the truth in love.

God is still speaking, as the United Church of Christ has been saying in their television spots for years. God is still speaking, but we're not always listening on the right frequency or in the right sanctuary, and sometimes we're just sound asleep.

God is speaking, in whispers and shouts, all around us. Kids are growing up without substantive support in school, or anybody who really cares what they do after the last bell rings. The ranting about health care that this country endured for months as Congress debated reform bills—the ranting that still continues on cable news shows—is an attempt to drown out other voices crying for help and healing and hope for wholeness. I seem to remember the disciples trying to hush more than one such person, but Jesus always cut through the protests and heard their voices anyway. How are the leaders in our communities of faith helping to give those voices a hearing?

There was a wonderful vignette in the September 18, 2007, issue of *The Christian Century*, about the pastor of a church in a town where skateboarding was against the law. The kids did it anyway, and they were treated as juvenile delinquents. That pastor decided to build a skate park in the church's backyard and discovered an abundant harvest. She poured out her heart and her creativity, and the gospel flourished in that improvised skateboard park.

The ministry that all Christians share is supposed to be kenotic. That's shorthand for "given away." It's a word that's most often used to talk about how God was poured out, becoming human in Jesus, or in Jesus emptying his life on the cross, or in the way that Jesus lived among us, without resort to the protections of force, family, or a stable home or political position.

Roland Allen, a clergyman who worked in China in the late 1800s and wrote extensively about his experience, reminded us of what kenotic ministry looks like in a mission context. He said the job of the evangelist is to give the scriptures and the sacraments and get out of the way. That's what Jesus does in sending laborers out into the harvest with good news and healing (Matthew 9:35–38), and it's what the Apostle Paul did in founding communities around the Mediterranean. He kept in touch by letter, but he didn't stick around to ensure uniformity in each community.

Roland Allen is a perpetual reminder that the traditions and habits and church's ways of doing things—which we think are absolutely central—are sometimes just ornate decorations that prevent us from seeing the face of a lost child. And sometimes those things are the noise that keeps us from hearing the voice of God calling us in the middle of the night.

We live in an urgent time, with fields filled with abundant gifts for helping others, and filled with desperate need for the good news and healing those gifts can offer. How can we do our best listening?

I've been blown away by the grace of some of our departing staff at The Episcopal Church Center—people whose positions have disappeared in this budget era. They readied others to take over their ministry, helping to shape the way forward, and truly building up the body in love, quite literally giving away their ministry into other hands or other bodies.

I am aware of similar ministry in other places throughout the church as well, as people of faith have stood up and spoken the truth they knew, truth that was often painful to hear, truth that may have had uncomfortable consequences. Any faith community that seeks to grow must learn something about listening to those unexpected voices, sometimes crying in the wilderness.

The work of ministry we all share is about truth telling and self-emptying. I think it is the Franciscans who speak of that work in this fourfold way: show up, pay attention, tell the truth, and leave the results to God.

Those are our marching orders, too: Keep showing up, even and especially in places that aren't obviously "church." Show up and listen deeply to the hurts and pains of a broken world. Tell the truth of what we hear and what we know—speak good news to the world's bad news. Give thanks for the healing that is going on, and keep challenging the world around us to listen. We must all do our part, and leave the ultimate healing to God.

We must keep listening, all of us, for that call from God in the middle of the night.

For Reflection

How have you discerned God's call to reach out to those in need?

Creative Survival

But Ruth said, "Do not press me to leave you or to turn back from following you! Where you go, I will go; where you lodge, I will lodge; your people shall be my people, and your God my God."

—RUTH 1:16

The story of Ruth and Naomi in the Hebrew Scriptures is about two women on their own—a precarious situation in the ancient world, and it could probably only be made into a movie if it carried an X rating. Naomi is out to procure a husband for her widowed daughter-in-law, Ruth—that's the only way either one of them can survive economically in a society where family connections are everything. She says to Ruth, "Look, there's Boaz—he's good husband material. Go get gussied up, then get yourself over to the barnyard, hang around, and show yourself off. Don't make yourself known to him until after dinner, but find out where he sleeps." (The verb "to know" has the same meaning as "and Adam knew his wife and she conceived and bore a child.")

When she's figured out Boaz's sleeping arrangements, Naomi tells her daughter-in-law to hightail it over there and "uncover his feet"—another euphemism—and to lie down beside him and let nature take its course.

Naomi is a very canny widow. She knows that she and Ruth won't survive if they don't have a male family member—a wage earner or a farmer—and they aren't going to get one without Ruth's cooperation. Julia Dinsmore, in *My Name Is Child of God ... Not "Those People": A First Person Look at Poverty*, would call this an example of "the survival skills of the poor."[1] It's a powerful illustration of the gifts of the poor, particularly their creativity.

We tend to judge this story from a very different economic location—one that offers us the luxury of at least some choice about what kind of work we'll take or who we'll marry or not marry. And if we read further in this story of creative survival, we discover that God is at work in the midst of it, for Ruth and Boaz marry, and eventually she becomes great-grandmother to David, the hoped-for savior and king of Israel. When David doesn't pan out so well, God keeps on working. Ruth shows up in Jesus' list of ancestors, along with three other women: the prostitute Rahab; Tamar, a widow who procures sons by seducing her father-in-law; and another foreigner, Bathsheba, with whom David commits adultery, and then makes a widow. God is at work in all of this "inappropriate sexual behavior," which eventually, according to Matthew's gospel, leads to Jesus, born of Mary, husband of Joseph of the house of David (Matthew 1:1–16).

This story continues, through all the centuries since, with more Naomis and Ruths, desperately looking for hope, in every part of the world.

Edward Ball's *Slaves in the Family* is about the black and white descendants of the Ball family, who started the big slave plantations outside Charleston, South Carolina.[2] There are a whole lot of arranged marriages in the Ball family. On the white side, most of them are with cousins, to keep the "property" in the family. Many of the marriages in the black community are arranged by slave masters who decide which slaves will marry whom. There are uncouplings and widow-makings as well, as slaves are sold off the plantation. And then there are the relationships between sons of the masters—or the masters themselves—and the women in slavery. Edward Ball learns about much of this family history by reading the slave records and connecting them with the family stories he hears from his black relatives. The surprising reality is that there wasn't a whole lot of choice about who married whom on either side of the family—and women were usually on the short end of the decision making. Ruth and Naomi's story is universal.

That's really what Jesus is getting at when he talks about the poor widow who gave her mite at the temple (Mark 12:41–44). This gospel story isn't so much an ode to her generosity as it is a condemnation of the religious leaders who "devour widows' houses," demanding their last few pennies and exploiting their lack of freedom to make economic decisions. The widows of Jesus' day were in just as wretched a social position as Ruth and Naomi had been hundreds of years earlier. They couldn't make it economically without a wage earner in the family. In Jesus' day, there were no jobs or economic possibilities for poor women without male relatives—except, of course, for "the oldest profession."

The religious leaders of first-century Palestine were the scribes who interpreted the laws of the Hebrew Scriptures—they played a role similar to the rabbis in the years after Jesus, as interpreters of scripture for daily life. In this passage in Mark, Jesus criticizes them for getting rich off those poor widows. Their legal deals and interpretations just keep squeezing the poor.

That's probably what lies behind Jesus' comments about the widow and her two coins. He notes the difference between the rich folk who give lots of money and the widow who gives her last two pennies. In order to be a good Jew in Jesus' day, you had to make an offering at the Temple. In order to keep the Romans off your back, you also had to pay Roman taxes. This widow is giving the very last of what she has. We don't know if she's motivated by gratitude or by a desire to maintain her social standing. But Jesus doesn't praise her. He simply notes that she's giving the last of what she has. His comments are a critique of a religious system that keeps widows poor by depriving them of economic possibilities and any real hope.

Recently, I visited Emmaus House, in a historically African American community in Atlanta, Georgia, where staff members and volunteers provide hope by offering tutoring, art classes, a senior citizen group, meals, and guidance and assistance for the poor at their Poverty Rights Office. While I was there, I met with the urban interns—three young women, recent college graduates who are spending a year working with some of today's equivalents of Ruth and Naomi and the poor widows of Jesus' day. They are working with other young women without much hope or economic freedom of choice, young women who are being trafficked or groomed for exploitation. The interns are supported and encouraged by older women and men who are trying to change a system that seduces poor young women into relationships for the profit of others, who are today's equivalent of slave holders and devourers of widows' houses.

All the sin in these stories—the story of Ruth and Naomi, the story of the poor widow, the story of the young women without hope and choice today—is really about removing creative possibility from others, denying them their God-given ability to make choices, to exercise their free will. That is what is most essential about being created in the image of God—sharing in God's own creativity. Ruth and Naomi didn't have much opportunity to choose another way because their society limited them to specific roles. Jesus' other female ancestors were similarly limited. The widow of the gospel is kept poor by a religious and political system of exploitation. The same was true of the Ball family—with the women on both sides of the plantation mightily constrained by the system. Fear of loss and poverty motivated the slave owners, and fear of death and destruction and further degradation kept most of the slaves in the system. Many young people today are being raised in a system that says that they have value only for the ways in which they can be used—by tricks on the corner or by athletic teams or by the military.

But the freedom we have in Jesus is about hope. Jesus' way insists that all God's people are created for dignity, and each one has meaning and value from being made in the image of God. No one is a commodity to be bought and sold.

Each one of us shares in Jesus' work of confronting the scribes who diminish dignity and steal hope. Opportunities for redemption are all around us, in the young and the old. God is at work even in the worst and most desperate places. Our job is to help give birth to hope, and help it keep growing into full and abundant life.

Let there be no more days when hope unborn has died. We must garner all the riches of creativity to lift every voice for those who are suffering. We must sing hope, bring hope, birth hope. We must be people of hope.

For Reflection

What are some of the hopeless places in your community, in your life? How can you bring God's hope to create change?

Opening Doors to Women

When the day of Pentecost had come, they were all together in one place. And suddenly from heaven there came a sound like the rush of a violent wind, and it filled the entire house where they were sitting. Divided tongues, as of fire, appeared among them, and a tongue rested on each of them. All of them were filled with the Holy Spirit and began to speak in other languages, as the Spirit gave them ability.

—ACTS 2:1–4

Women have come a long way in the church and in the world in the last twenty years, and we have a long way yet to go. We have seen doors unlocked, and hills climbed, and the blind healed. But there are still plenty of locks bolted shut, lots of people who refuse to see, and more rocky roads to be trod.

The psalmist says, "I will lift up my eyes to the hills, from where is my help to come?" (Psalm 121:1; Book of Common Prayer). Human beings have always looked to the heights, sometimes for the cavalry or a prince on a white horse to come and rescue them. Even we church folk are never quite sure whether to understand that psalm as a question or a statement: "Where will I find help?" or "I know it's up there!" Christians lift up their eyes and see Jesus, hanging on a cross, reminding us that salvation is to be found in solidarity with the lowliest and most rejected. In much of the world, those are women and children.

We still live in a world where schools that try to teach girls are attacked, their students scarred with acid and their teachers murdered. Children in the United States are still sometimes confined against their will in so-called religious reeducation camps, usually run by extremely conservative Christian groups who use force to make children comply with what male and mostly white leaders teach as divinely inspired truth. The Anglican Church of Canada has apologized for that kind of behavior in residential schools, but The Episcopal Church in the U.S. has not yet done so. Until we live in a world where the God-given gifts of each—regardless of gender—can be offered for the well-being of all, we will continue to lift up our eyes to the hills.

I love hills—more specifically, mountains. I've spent my life wanting to climb up there and see what was going on in the larger world. Women who have blazed trails ahead of us—including Barbara Harris, an African American and the first woman bishop in The Episcopal Church—have spent their lives trusting in the God who makes those hills, certain that a level road will eventually appear, a road that is accessible to all. Barbara has been climbing up and down hills her whole life—beginning with her travels through the Jim Crow South, where her journeys were almost always uphill. And her journeying has done a great deal to bulldoze the human-built hills within and beyond the church.

I got my first taste of what those human hills are like when my family moved to a new town in New Jersey. I started at a new school in the middle of eighth grade, and when my mother took me to the office to sign me up for classes, I heard about the electives that cycled through the year—wood shop, metal shop, cooking, sewing, and art. I wanted to take wood shop—and I was furious when I was told that girls couldn't do that. I knew how to saw boards and pound nails, but I wanted to learn how to use a lathe. I'd spent the first part of my childhood in a girls' school in Seattle where there weren't any overt limits on what girls could study or try.

A month or so later, as I was getting my books out of my locker to go home at the end of the day, a group of black girls came down the hall with their arms linked, sweeping everyone else out of the way. They were clearly very angry, but I had no idea why. I must have said something about the incident in English class, because my teacher suggested that I write a paper on the Ku Klux Klan. I discovered a world of evil and violence that revolted and horrified me. I was only eleven or twelve, but I got a powerful sense of the forces that work to keep the world off balance. I knew that at the very least the scales of justice weren't supposed to operate like that, and that God had a different dream for the way human beings were meant to live.

The kind of fear behind the KKK and Jim Crow and white-men-only clubs doesn't just lock doors and kill people. It takes away basic human dignity from everyone. It denies the image of God, both in those who are feared and in those who bar the doors. The first disciples locked their own door after Jesus' execution. Forgetting everything he'd taught them about healing and feeding and loving the enemy, they hid together, afraid that the authorities would come and execute them, too. But we cannot do the same, as hard as some people may try to chain those doors shut.

When I was growing up, the doors of the sacristy (the room in the church where the items for church services are stored) were locked to everyone but the altar guild—the ladies in the parish who tended to the linens and flowers and communion vessels. And even they had to put doilies on their heads before they could venture inside. They certainly weren't allowed to unbolt the vestment closet and put on the robes that priests wear to celebrate the sacraments.

In much the same way, the doors of countless hotels and restaurants were barred to African Americans such as Barbara Harris as they traveled around the South in the years before the Civil Rights Act, and I expect a fair number of doors were politely but conveniently closed north of the Mason-Dixon line as well. But the doors of the church were flung open the day Barbara carried the cross down the aisle in 1974 for the ordination of the first eleven women as priests in The Episcopal Church. And try as some might to prevent it, the people of the church again unlocked the doors when she herself was consecrated as a bishop in 1989. Collectively, The Episcopal Church looked to the hills and discovered that our fears were sitting in the pew with us, and our help was to be found in the midst of us, wherever two or three or a thousand were gathered.

In too many places, though, the doors are still locked. The Church of England is wrestling mightily to open the episcopal door, to allow women to serve as bishops. They're not willing to simply take the door off the hinges, like we restless Americans tend to do. They're trying to pick a thousand tiny locks, one at a time, forgetting that a woman has gotten through the door by another way, to sit at the head of the church—twice! The English queen may wear a different kind of hat than a bishop's miter, but it is the hat of respected and authorized leadership. An Englishman remarked to me recently that he thought the difficulty with female bishops in Britain was that British men didn't want to be under the authority of women. Well, in England they have accepted the leadership of Elizabeth II—one of her many titles is "Defender of the Faith"—for more than fifty years.

The doors aren't fully open here in the U.S., either. When silence or ruse or passing yourself off as straight is the only way through for some, those doors are still effectively closed. But closed doors shouldn't stop us. Jesus walks through anyway, as he did on Easter evening, and through his example he bids us follow. "Peace be with you," he says, and we're supposed to remember what the godly messenger always adds: "Fear not."

That peace that Jesus offers comes at a price—he shows us the wounds of his crucifixion—but it is a price that leads to life. Barbara

Harris has been paying that price for some eighty years, and other trailblazers have been paying it as well. Their grace and wit and humor have buoyed up the church—and inspired women of faith from all traditions. They've led others through the closed doors once they found the chinks. Those openings have most to do with confronting and engaging the fear that locks the doors in the first place.

Humor will often help pry those doors apart, and blunt words can be a wedge to keep them open. The skunk at the garden party has let others come inside, and the whole place smells a good deal better because of it.

The persistence and the unflagging and prophetic insistence of women of faith is an encouraging witness to all of us, in and beyond the church. The women in Uruguay who cannot be ordained priests or bishops look to our example. So do the women in African nations who eat in the kitchen because it's expected, after they serve their guests in the formal room. When they see women eating with the men, they get uppity ideas—the kind of ideas that begin to open doors for themselves, their sisters, and their daughters—and ultimately bring the peaceful society Jesus claimed.

Barbara Harris, the world's first Anglican female bishop, once admitted in a sermon, "I couldn't change that old-boys club by myself. It was important that other women be elected so those changes could take place. It's like eating an elephant, one bite at a time. The job isn't done yet. The elephant is yet to be consumed."

That elephant needs to be on more menus—the kind of menus that start with bread and wine and tears and solidarity and rejoicing, for one more door pried open.

"How beautiful upon the mountains are the feet of the messenger who announces peace, who brings good news" (Isaiah 52:7). This Hebrew prophet proclaimed renewed hope and a changed world. As we work for justice for all who are oppressed, remember that God's peace is with us, and our help is on the way.

For Reflection

What doors have you seen bolted shut in your own experience? How were they pried open?

Seeking Our Roots

*What good is it, my brothers and sisters, if you say you have
faith but do not have works? Can faith save you? If a brother or
sister is naked and lacks daily food, and one of you says to them,
"Go in peace; keep warm and eat your fill," and yet you do not
supply their bodily needs, what is the good of that? So faith by
itself, if it has no works, is dead. But someone will say, "You have
faith and I have works." Show me your faith apart from your
works, and I by my works will show you my faith.*

—JAMES 2:14–18

God has been at work in Americans of African descent in many
contexts. The God who promised to bring the slaves out of
Egypt has been invoked in other places of slavery, and the history of
slavery in the United States has connections to slavery in other
places around the world.

The largest diocese of The Episcopal Church is in Haiti. Before
the devastating earthquake there in January 2010, Bishop Jean Zaché
Duracin reported that there were some 120,000 Episcopalians, in 169
congregations, served by 37 clergy under his spiritual care. That
diocese ran 254 schools, serving 80,000 students, from preschool to
university, as well as a school for handicapped children, trade and
music schools, and the only graduate nursing school in the nation.
All that work owes its beginning to James Theodore Holly, one of
the first African American priests of The Episcopal Church, who was

ordained in Connecticut in 1856. He also helped start the Protestant Episcopal Society for Promoting the Extension of the Church Among Colored People, which eventually gave rise to today's Union of Black Episcopalians.

After serving for several years as a rector at St. Luke's in New Haven, Connecticut, Holly left the United States in 1861 with a hundred others, to settle in Haiti. One of the first things he did there was to start a school, so that potential converts might be able to read the Bible. He founded Holy Trinity Church, which later became the cathedral of the Diocese of Haiti, destroyed in the 2010 earthquake. In 1874 he became the bishop of Haiti, the first African American bishop in The Episcopal Church. Twenty years later he also became the bishop of the Dominican Republic, and he served both dioceses until he died in 1911.

When we look a bit more deeply at the history of Haiti we can see more of the ties that bind us together. Established in 1804 as the second free and independent nation in the Western Hemisphere, Haiti was born of a slave revolt against France. The people of Haiti had honed their hopes for freedom by the example offered by the American War of Independence. In 1779, a number of Haitians fought on behalf of our emerging nation in the Battle of Savannah. Haiti was also significantly involved in other revolutions in Latin America, helping Venezuelan military leader Simon Bolivar with funds and soldiers in establishing five other sovereign nations independent of their European colonial masters.

The links between Haiti and the United States continued as well. Many Haitians settled in New Orleans during and after the slave rebellions there, and a good deal of New Orleans culture has its roots in Haiti. The history of oppression is shared, and the similarities between the effects of Katrina and the recent earthquake are not accidental. God's people are still groaning in the wilderness.

Father Holly was not the first or only free black American to seek greater freedom and self-determination in Haiti. Many abolitionists in the United States believed that resettling free blacks in other places would help solve the problem of slavery in the U.S. and provide greater opportunities for freed blacks, away from the pervasive racism in this country. The motives of those colonization initiatives were not always the highest—some advocates thought exporting the problem was more expeditious than curing this nation of the ills of slavery.

A similar colonization initiative led to the establishment of the African nation of Liberia, which was a diocese of The Episcopal Church until 1982. The American Colonization Society sent free black settlers to the coast of West Africa in the early 1820s, leading to the establishment of Liberia as a free nation in 1836. The government of Kentucky was among those who provided funds for transportation. The first colonists were followed by Episcopal missionaries. Though many of them died of disease soon after they landed, the work they began took root and flourished. The American colonists became the ruling class in Liberia, and it was the native Africans who eventually began to cry out for deliverance from their second-class status. The civil wars of the last decades in Liberia are the result.

These United States have, over the centuries, attempted to keep both nations in thrall as client states, through dominance of the sugar industry in Haiti and the rubber industry in Liberia. Our armed forces have been called on to "keep order," and our government has attempted to maintain conditions favorable to American business interests. We have some lasting responsibility for the cries in the wilderness in both places.

At the same time, The Episcopal Church has been a major resource for education and health care in both nations, answering needs their governments have been unable to fill. The Diocese of Liberia opened the first degree-granting educational institution in Africa, Cuttington University, in 1889, with a grant from the treasurer of The Episcopal Church. Before the civil wars in Liberia, nearly half of all government officials were graduates of Cuttington.

In recent years the United States has received a number of Haitian and Liberian migrants, with a resulting expansion and enrichment of African American culture. The migration crosses our borders in both directions. Hilda Alcindor, who started that graduate nursing school in Haiti, spent thirty years here in the U.S., then went home to share her gifts. The current president of Cuttington University, Henrique Tokpa, received his doctorate in the U.S. So did many of the Liberian Episcopalians who are today's government ministers, and leaders in education, politics, and business.

The call of the gospel is to love God with all we are and have, and to love our neighbors as ourselves. Our brothers and sisters of African heritage in The Episcopal Church continue to lead us toward a world where cries in the wilderness are heard and answered. We are edified, built up, encouraged, and challenged by the witness of these saints, fellow members of the body of Christ.

In the Hebrew Scriptures, Moses was called to lead God's people out of slavery in Egypt into the promised land. Some of those former slaves arrived only to find out that they were meant to do a lot of the work of grounding the promise. They had glimpses of the promise, and some seasons in their history seemed closer to the promise than others.

But that promised land is still waiting, for each of us. If we're all going to get across the river, past the rocks and the snakes, the crooks and the warlords, we're going to have to love our neighbors. None of us will find our home, our true native land, until we all do. The promised land requires the healing of the whole of God's family. We are all related, under the skin. We have learned in recent years that our DNA has its common origin in Africa—we all have African ancestors, even if some are very far away and long ago. We have the same source, the same creator, and the same destiny. We give thanks for Africa, cradle of humanity. We give thanks for the gospel witness of African American saints, leading us onward to the promised land, the garden that God has given to us all.

For Reflection

We can discover our connectedness to others only by engaging them in holy conversation. How have conversations connected you to others?

Peace Work

Peace I leave with you; my peace I give to you. I do not give to you as the world gives. Do not let your hearts be troubled and do not be afraid.

—JOHN 14:27

A t a week-long bishops' meeting in Texas, we spent most of the Sunday in Sabbath rest. One of the recreational offerings was horseback riding. A number of bishops went for a trail ride—a very sedate excursion, with gentle and slow-walking horses and not much excitement. Even so, the next day I heard a couple of bishops talking about how sore they were. That kind of unaccustomed exercise stretches muscles that aren't used much, but the pain and discomfort is a sign of greater life—it's the result of new or renewed joy.

When Jesus finally makes his way into Jerusalem for the last time, he's not taking unaccustomed exercise—he's doing what he's been preparing for his whole life. He's going to challenge the empire of Caesar and his minions (Luke 19:28–40). He's going to insist that God's kingdom is the greater, and that God's reign is one of peace and abundant justice for all, not just a few powerful human beings who exploit and subject others for their own ends.

There's all sorts of symbolism and political freight wrapped up in this parade into Jerusalem, because a lot of Jews expected to be rescued by a powerful military king. When his disciples bring back a mount, Jesus is offered an unridden and untamed colt. The expectation was for the kind of king who would come riding in at the head of an army. This king is supposed to ride a war stallion, a great and powerful beast intended to dominate and frighten. In other gospel accounts Jesus rides a donkey—a sign of humility, and maybe an echo of the same animal that the pregnant Mary rode. At the end of his life, he leaves on the same animal that helped bring him into this world.

But this unridden horse says something else. An unridden and unbroken horse usually bucks its rider off pretty quickly. It's unlikely to walk sedately down the street, especially a road covered with jackets and coats and capes that have been thrown in its way. It's much more likely that this horse is going to shy away, buck off its rider, and run off into the crowd. Does riding this horse say something about Jesus' internal struggle? He knows something about what's waiting for him there in the city, even if he's unsure of the details, but he's not going to run back to the barn.

Horses are remarkably sensitive to the emotional state of their riders. A fearful rider can't get a horse over a challenging jump, and a nervous cowpoke will never get his pony to stand still while he tries to rope and tie a calf. Remember how the character Tom Booker in *The Horse Whisperer* befriended and gentled intractable mounts? Luke paints us a picture of something like that with Jesus and this horse. This isn't about violent control—Jesus doesn't beat this horse into submission. This isn't a war horse, chained down and held in so it's safe enough to ride through the streets.

This is about Jesus exercising all his muscles—physical, emotional, and spiritual muscles—in the ride of his life. He's exercising those muscles in relaxing and giving up anxiety, in remembering that there is nothing to fear. This truly is the king of peace, the kind of peace that is willing to walk into the jaws of death for the sake of abundant life.

Today that king of peace rides in earthquake-torn Haiti, and in the conflict in Sudan. That king rides through the streets of Mexico, and the Dominican Republic, and Omaha and Atlanta—into court-rooms and classrooms and living rooms where people struggle to find a life of peace. We go there, too, when we're willing to confront the fear and violence of broken human communities.

Peace isn't about total relaxation. It's about giving up fear and doing the hard work of confronting evil. That's what Jesus means when he says that if his followers are silenced, even the stones will cry out (Luke 19:40). God intends peace, and all creation will con-spire with the word of God that speaks peace.

Where will we find the king of peace today? I suspect that the king of peace will turn up in Haiti, living in a tent with people who have been displaced by the earthquake. We can probably find him living and working with pregnant teens in Omaha, and with immi-grants struggling to learn enough English to stand up for their rights under new laws that target the undocumented. He sits and waits with people everywhere who die too young because they haven't had adequate health care. Do you hear the king of peace coming when people cry out and insist on justice, in order that God's glory may be evident? Following Jesus on the road may take us to Calvary and the cross, but we will find joy and peace and more abundant life on that blessed road.

That's what the crowds are saying along Jesus' path as he makes his way into Jerusalem: "Peace in heaven and glory to God." May your path be blessed, they are saying, and may the peace of heaven come on earth; may God's kingdom come quickly. We know another version in the cowpoke's blessing, "Happy trails," wishing a blessed road to all who pass. Our road is made happy or blessed by the com-panionship of one who rides into Jerusalem and walks the road to Calvary.

Our invitation at the gates of Jerusalem is to join in making the trail a blessing for all. It means courageous response to evil and injus-tice, using all the muscles we've been given—including the ones that don't get exercised very often. Will we cry out for peace? Will we speak up for just treatment of all God's children? Will we minister to the suffering of brothers and sisters in our neighborhoods and around the world? That way lies the kingdom of God.

We pray for happy trails, even if they lead through the valley of the shadow of death. Fear not, our faith tells us. Jesus rides with us. Will we ride with him?

For Reflection

Where will we follow Jesus into the face of fear? Where will we exercise our spiritual muscle by giving up anxiety and entering into the peace that passes understanding?

Part Two

Connecting Faith with Public Life

The Christian Scriptures letter of James sums it up: "So faith by itself, if it has no works, is dead" (James 2:17). Another way of saying it is that we can't love God if we don't love our neighbors as we love ourselves. Our faith has to have consequences for the way in which we live our daily lives—at work, at play, with our next-door neighbors, in the voting booth, and on the highway. When we start to think about the issues involved in living together with other human beings, things such as health care and healing, how we use or use up the resources of this planet, and what kinds of civil and human rights we think are important, it's not too hard to see that those moral and ethical questions ought to be informed by the resources of faith. The Bible, our Christian tradition, and the best of human reason are all essential resources to connect us to the heart of God—which connects us to the hearts of our neighbors.

Immigration and Faith

The alien who resides with you shall be to you as the citizen among you; you shall love the alien as yourself, for you were aliens in the land of Egypt: I am the Lord your God.

—LEVITICUS 19:34

Christians understand that we are all aliens and sojourners, seeking our home in God. In a spiritual sense, we are all migrants. As Americans, we are a nation of immigrants. All of us, even Native peoples, originated as the human species evolved in Africa, and humanity has been migrating for tens or hundreds of thousands of years ever since. That migration is a persistent movement in search of food, shelter, safety, employment, and even adventure and discovery.

The current crisis of immigration policy in the United States stems primarily from economic and resource imbalances, and an exodus from poorer nations unable to sustain adequate opportunities for growing populations. That imbalance is complicated by violence—both terrorism and the drug trade—as well as by reduced employment opportunities within the United States.

Most Americans recognize the failure of our current migration policies, but there is a wide range of preferred solutions or appropriate political responses. The passage of Arizona's identification law is a recent and troubling expression of our national political failure.

The Episcopal Church has repeatedly expressed its position on immigration issues from a theological perspective. That theology begins in the biblical charge to love God and to love one's neighbor as oneself (Leviticus 19:18). The alien or foreigner is among the neighbors to be regarded with love and justice. Hebrew Scripture repeatedly (thirty-eight times!) directs the faithful to "care for the alien and sojourner in your midst." "You shall also love the stranger, for you were strangers in the land of Egypt" (Deuteronomy 10:19). That sense of having the shared experience of migration and being a foreigner opens us up to the shared reality of all humanity, and motivates us to find all sorts of partners who also understand that shared reality. It is a central way in which the religious motivation engages the political.

Theological responses to issues of migration are also based in Jesus' mandate to care for the "least of these"—the hungry, thirsty, homeless, sick, unemployed, oppressed, and imprisoned (Matthew 25:34–40). Anyone experiencing those realities is alienated from the state of healed and whole reality that we speak of as the kingdom of God—that ancient prophetic vision of a world of justice and peace often called *shalom*. Those who experience such alienation are also migrants, sojourners in search of healing and wholeness.

The Episcopal Church has been involved in work with refugees and migrants in a formal way since 1940, with the advent of Episcopal Migration Ministries. Today we resettle some four to five thousand migrants a year, in partnership with the federal government and local community agencies. We know something about successfully integrating newcomers.

The Episcopal Church is not only an American church. In addition to those in the United States, we have congregations in fifteen other nations, from Taiwan and Micronesia to Central and South America, the Caribbean, and Europe. Within the United States, our congregations include more than three hundred serving Latino immigrant communities—it is one of our fastest growing demographics—as well as immigrants from Sudan, Korea, Liberia, Vietnam, Haiti, the Philippines, Taiwan, Laos, and a number of other nations.

Our historical partnerships and covenant relationships with other Anglican churches around the world inform and challenge us to build just political systems in many nations. We strive to see that all human beings are treated with dignity and respect, whether they are Filipino guest workers in Saipan, migrant Latino farm workers in the United States, or Sudanese, Bolivian, and Afghani migrants in the city of Rome. Our congregations address the needs of these and many other groups of sojourners and immigrants.

The current thrust of our immigration advocacy work seeks dignity and justice for all. Our priorities are to provide legal entry opportunities for those seeking to respond to needs for labor, to normalize the status of out-of-status immigrants already here and provide routes to legal residency or citizenship, to reunify families, and to equalize the burden of enforcement so that it is humane and proportionate, all in the context of secure borders and reduced levels of fear and violence.

As a church, we are troubled by the impact of current immigration policies. On Good Friday 2010 in Phoenix, Arizona, local police stationed outside a church with a large Latino membership prevented many of those people from worshiping. We note the fear engendered by raids on workplaces—children live with daily anxiety that their parents won't be there when they come home from school. We are hampered as a church by an inability to find adequate numbers of effective leaders for immigrant congregations.

The bishops of our church met in Arizona in September 2010, a meeting that had been planned for several years. Our commitment to proceed with that meeting was a way of expressing solidarity with the Latino community and exposing the community of bishops to realities on the U.S.-Mexico border. A number of those bishops were temporary sojourners in the U.S., whose primary ministry is in another nation, and some are themselves immigrants to the United States. Members of the group were at some hazard themselves of being required to identify themselves while in Arizona. But we were there to make an on-site witness, through learning and accompaniment, as well as to express our concerns as a church. The Episcopal Church seeks justice, dignity, and equality in these matters, and we will continue to partner with any and all who share those values and priorities. We must never forget that we or our ancestors have been aliens ourselves and that God calls us to offer hospitality and justice to those who are sojourners among us today. Not a single American can claim to have become a citizen without the hospitality and justice-seeking of those who came before us.

For Reflection

Dealing with immigration reform demands that we confront our fears. Name the fears at work in our society, our neighborhoods, our congregations.

Salt of the Earth

You are the salt of the earth; but if salt has lost its taste, how can its saltiness be restored? It is no longer good for anything, but is thrown out and trampled under foot.

—MATTHEW 5:13

Most Americans would probably say that the average midwesterner is "salt of the earth." It conveys the understanding that good common sense abounds like wheat and corn in the American heartland, and that the people who live there won't be lured away by the excesses of some dubious enterprise or flagrantly seductive advertising. Yet the midwest is not exactly average. It's more like the mythical Lake Wobegon community Garrison Keillor celebrates, which turns cultural stereotypes upside down, where the men are good-looking, the women are strong, and all the children are above average. Midwesterners are all of these things and more.

Average or above average, handsome or strong, midwesterners or not, Jesus takes us wherever we start, and asks us to be appropriately salty. In the context of the gospel, we're not supposed to avoid the salt, for it is a sign of life—and it always has been. It's still a basic symbol of hospitality in the Middle East and on the steppes of Asia. It's often presented to visitors, along with bread, as a way of saying, "Your life is safe with us, and we recognize you as friend." That's actually what Jesus does for us, inviting us into friendship: "I call you friend, no longer do I call you servant, but friend" (John 15:15; my translation).

Where do we encounter the kind of salt that Jesus is talking about, that salt of welcome and friendship and life? Where does each of us find the salt in our own lives? Maybe it was the whiff of salt in the air along New York's East River on a recent morning, as the tide pushed in from the sea, but what I thought of first was the salt within all of us—the taste of salt in the tears my eyes were making in the cold wind, but also the taste of salt in blood and sweat. And our connection with the sea isn't trivial—seawater has a lot to do with the composition of the blood in our veins. The salt within us is indeed about life, for it reflects our evolutionary history, and our origins in a salty sea.

Salt was an ancient coin, a medium of exchange, because it's portable and reasonably stable—it only melts away in a rainstorm, and rainstorms aren't so common in the Middle East. Salt is a sign of value, and at some times and places it's been exchangeable, ounce for ounce, with gold.

The salty signs of blood, sweat, and tears remind us continually of the cost of life, and its preciousness. Jesus gave abundantly of all three, weeping at the death of a friend, sweating in the Garden of Gethsemane, and at the end giving up his blood along with his life. Blood, sweat, and tears are part of our own costly living, if we are to be truly alive. They are sacramental evidence of a compassionate heart.

That heart is what Jesus is asking his disciples for—a heart of flesh, fully alive, connected to other human beings and the whole of creation, a heart that can feel with and respond to the pain and joy of others. That's salt.

The value of salt was involved in the practice of seating some "above the salt" and others below, in the ranking of guests at a dinner party. Jesus' table, though, is effectively round, and the salt is in the center, at the heart. All his friends are equally welcome to share his meal of life—a meal with plenty of salt, in the bread and in the wine, and even a little in the water.

Salt has other resonances—consider, for example, a salty vocabulary, or *palabras saladas,* those earthy words our mothers discouraged us from using. That kind of salt gets attention, and when our audience is asleep, such language can be very useful. The biblical prophets used the ancient equivalent of salty words all the time: "You cows of Bashan, lolling around on ivory couches, while your neighbors are starving on your doorstep" (Amos 4:1; my translation). John Baptist and Jesus did, too: "You brood of vipers" (Matthew 12:34), "you whitewashed tombs" (Matthew 23:27). Those salty words can indeed be divinely abrasive signs of God's urgency.

The letters we write to our members of Congress, or to the editor of the local paper, or the words we speak in a town meeting can be salt when they challenge a sleepy government to pay attention to the needs of hungry children or the unemployed. That is the salt of compassion—even though it may feel irritating to those who are invited to wake up to their neighbors' needs and demonstrate compassion.

Like all good gifts, salt can be overused—and the excessive use of a good gift often leads to counterintuitive results. Salt is a very good preservative, and we still use it to make things such as ham and pickles. But too much salt in our food also pickles *us*—and leads to less of life, rather than more. Excessively salty critique may end a relationship and the possibility of change. When our conversation partners shut down in the face of abrasive words, the agony of the situation is simply fixed, frozen in place, until healing balm or the water of grace or even the purification of salt tears help signs of life emerge once more.

In addition to being the salt of the earth, Jesus also asks us to be the light of the world (Matthew 5:14). Salt is actually necessary to make light. Salts—and there are lots of kinds of salts—are merely charged particles, ions, that generate an action or a reaction. Whether it's the fiery energy of the sun, the light from a battery or an outlet, or even the light from a firefly, the production of light depends on something salty. If we are to become light to the world and show what God looks like in human form, we're going to have to be appropriately salty.

Our task is to figure out where and how. What's cooking in our faith communities right now? What needs signs of life, and good news? Health-care reform, unemployment, caring for our neighbors? Anti-gay propagandist Fred Phelps and the members of the Westboro Baptist Church in Topeka, Kansas, continue to demonstrate around the country, preaching their message of hate toward gay people. That hateful message just might be addressed by being entombed in a pillar of salt—like Lot's wife, who hesitates as they flee from Sodom, which God aims to destroy for its abysmal lack of hospitality (Genesis 19:20–26). Burying something in salt is a method of purification or protection, like our government's plans to bury nuclear waste in old salt mines in Nevada. That stuff certainly isn't life-giving, so we salt it away until it decomposes.

How and where will we use our salt?

Sometimes it only takes the tiniest pinch of salt to transform a life. The woman who cuts my hair is a Brazilian immigrant. She's been here more than twenty years, and she speaks English pretty well. Last spring she told me she could read English reasonably well, but she couldn't write it. She wanted to learn, but she couldn't afford the tuition. I went back to the office and did a little digging. First I tried the local churches, but none of them had English as a Second Language (ESL) classes—and this in New York City, where every other person seems to be an immigrant! The next time I saw her I told her I hadn't had any luck. Then it dawned on me that there must be other resources in the community. A quick Google search turned up the Office of Adult and Continuing Education in New York City, which offers ESL classes for free. I printed off the brochure, and a list of the locations where these classes are offered. When I took these two measly sheets of paper to her, she absolutely lit up—she was ecstatic!

The last time I saw her, she told me that she is in love with the Saturday computer course she's also taking. She also told me that her English teacher thinks she'll be able to pass her GED exam pretty soon and receive her high school equivalency diploma. Eventually, I expect she'll find significantly better employment—and I'll probably have to find another person to cut my hair. But, oh, what light she radiates, every time I see her!

Following Jesus means using our blood, sweat, and tears, and in the process becoming light to a dark and distracted world.

For Reflection

Where will you spend your salt to spread the zest and flavor of the gospel? How will your salt help produce more light in this world?

Heaven on Earth

When Jesus saw the crowds, he went up the mountain; and after he sat down, his disciples came to him. Then he began to speak, and taught them, saying:

"Blessed are the poor in spirit,
   for theirs is the kingdom of heaven.
Blessed are those who mourn,
   for they will be comforted.
Blessed are the meek,
   for they will inherit the earth.
Blessed are those who hunger and thirst for righteousness,
   for they will be filled.
Blessed are the merciful,
   for they will receive mercy.
Blessed are the pure in heart,
   for they will see God.
Blessed are the peacemakers,
   for they will be called children of God.
Blessed are those who are persecuted for righteousness's sake,
   for theirs is the kingdom of heaven."

—MATTHEW 5:1–10

What's your image of the kingdom of heaven? What would the world look like if everything were healed and reconciled? Where would you start?

Stop the wars. Cure the disease that's killing your friend. Make sure that kids everywhere grow up with plenty of adults who care about them, and schools that nurture and challenge their gifts. Build adequate houses for everybody in Haiti—and on every reservation in South Dakota and in every Appalachian cove and holler. Make sure that everybody has enough to eat, and enough for a little feasting once in a while. Bless all adults with meaningful opportunities to put their gifts to work, in ways that are adequate to support their families. Heal the earth and its creatures—clean up the fouled air and water, including the oil spill in the Gulf of Mexico, restore the denuded and decapitated mountains, and figure out how to turn the stuff we call garbage into a blessing.

When we start to look at the particulars, it's easier to see how interconnected all the pieces of this dream are. We're not going to find decent and meaningful employment for everybody unless we figure out how to share more of the abundance that God has already provided. Sufficient numbers of good schools and health care for everybody both depend on a more equitable economic and political system. If we destroy the garden we aren't going to be able to feed everyone. And before we go too far down the line of things we dream about, remember that wars usually get fought over resources—land and what it holds or represents.

When Jesus and the prophets before him proclaim a vision of the kingdom of heaven or the reign of God, they're talking about all these interrelated realities. That's what all the language is about— water in the desert, comfort for the grieving, strong hands and firm knees, sight for the blind and hearing for the deaf, and a straight road home through the terror of the wilderness.

Our faith encourages us to dream dreams, to remember who we are, and whose we are, and where we're going.

That dream has much to do with realizing that God loves all that is—poor people as well as wealthy ones, folks here in the United States and in Bangladesh, and all the rest of creation, not just people.

God intends all creation to flourish, not for some to get fat on others' privation. Yet we human beings love to divide up the world into categories of privileged and shunned. The kingdom of heaven doesn't have room for that.

That's a good part of what it means to be poor in spirit—those folks that Jesus says are blessed with the kingdom of heaven (Matthew 5:3). If you're poor in spirit, you're not lording it over somebody else; you're not playing those games of in and out, acceptable and despicable, better and worse. It's sort of like getting a bronze medal in the Olympics. You're just thankful for making it to the medal stand. The silver medalists are the ones who seem to have more trouble—they want to know why they didn't get the gold.

Jesus also blesses the folks who are attacked for trying to build that dream of God's: Blessed are you, he says, who are persecuted for your right sense of relationship (Matthew 5:10–12). These are the people who ask the challenging questions, such as why our country can't manage to provide even minimal health care for everyone, when other developed nations can do it—and do it far more cheaply and with better outcomes. And those obnoxious questions about why some people get treated differently, even though we insist that all are created equal.

As Christians, we believe that dream is the reason we are here. This kingdom of heaven work is what we've been sent to do. It's the mission of the church, but even more clearly, it's God's mission. It is the reason God sent Jesus—to heal divisions, and repair the breach, and fix what's broken between God and human beings. For people of faith, community is a tool for doing that work—it's a body equipped to dream the dream and live it. The Church—the body of Christ—is a dreamworks. Dreamworks is not movie director Steven Spielberg's monopoly, though he is very good at showing people what the ancient dream means—people and alien creatures of many different sorts struggling to live together in peace.

The dream begins in loving God with all you are and all you have, and loving your neighbor as yourself (Deuteronomy 6:5). The first part means that we recognize that all we have and are is gift, from the size of our feet (basketball or ballet?) to the passions we have (teaching children to read, organic farming, working for peace?). And the second part, loving neighbor as self, means joyfully putting those passions to work to begin to make the dream of God a reality.

Faith communities exist to help people dream the dream and begin to live it. Blessed are those who get past the fear that there won't be enough to go around, and blessed are those who yearn for a healed world, hungering and thirsting for restored relationships—their yearning will be answered.

How do you dream? In The Episcopal Church, a Reading Camp program has changed lives from Kentucky to South Africa to Liberia and Kenya. A ministry called Pyramid Professional Resources helps homeless and marginally housed people in Louisville, Kentucky, find work by providing bus passes, job counseling, resume coaching, and computer classes. Faith communities all over the country have worked to bridge the gulf between us and Haiti, and to provide assistance to those who have been devastated by the earthquake there.

It's usually fear that keeps us from dreaming God's dream. What are we afraid of? That fear in each of us is healed by recognizing how well we are loved, and that others are also exceedingly well loved.

Blessed are those who dream dreams with the heart of God—for they will indeed see that dream become reality. Blessed are the humble and poor in spirit, for theirs is the kingdom of heaven, in Minnesota and Florida, Alaska and Maine.

For Reflection

What part of the dream of God challenges you? What keeps you from engaging it?

Blessed Are the Change Makers

Consider how to provoke one another to love and good deeds.
—HEBREWS 10:24

Years ago, my husband and I were sitting in church, a couple of pews back from our friend Bruce, his son, and our five-year-old daughter. When it came time for the Lord's Prayer, Bruce challenged the two children to see who could say it the loudest. They stood on the kneelers, bouncing up and down, and egged each other on until they were shouting, "FORGIVE US OUR TRESPASSES, and LEAD US NOT INTO TEMPTATION." I wonder if that's what the writer of the letter to the Hebrews means when he says: "Consider how to provoke one another to love and good deeds" (Hebrews 10:24). I remember being both mortified that my child was part of this spectacle and trying not to laugh out loud.

Provoking love and good deeds often elicits complex reactions. We know we're supposed to act in loving ways, but changing our behavior can be pretty doggone hard. I think we can all agree that healing sick people is a good idea, but figuring out how to ensure that everybody in this country has access to health care is a lot tougher. We hope for a better world, but when we're faced with some of the realities that lie between that hope and what we see around us, we quail and tremble and sometimes give up.

That's what Jesus is talking about in Mark's gospel, when he proclaims what we've come to call the Beatitudes. It's a fancy word for "the Blessings"—blessed are the meek, the persecuted, the poor in spirit. Living in that blessed way, Jesus insists, is the way to love God and our neighbor—and those are the only rules that really count.

All of us try to avoid change. It often seems threatening, and responding to it with inertia always seems a lot easier than constructive action. So when we're faced with a new challenge, we tend to revert to rules rather than address the human suffering on our doorstep. How many times have we heard, "Illegal aliens don't deserve health care (or welfare, or education, or you name it)"? But where does loving God and our neighbor enter in?

The fact that we live by rules—the ones we automatically employ to keep life a bit simpler and more efficient—isn't the problem. The problem is the content of the rules we choose. If those rules we live by are the summary about loving God and neighbor with all we've got, then maybe change isn't quite so threatening. But when the disciples talk about what a great building the temple is, Jesus warns them that it's all going to fall down. And then he tells them not to worry, not to be afraid, even if the collapse of the temple and all it represents looks like the end of the world. Don't be afraid of change, he insists. After all, it's really the beginning of God's new day.

Change itself isn't the problem; our fear and anxiety about it is. Death—the ultimate change—is coming, but there is no new life without it. If we want light in the darkness, we're going to have to change the burned-out light bulb, even if it's an heirloom from our grandmother. And if we want to see the kingdom of God, we need to figure out how to change enough to start feeding the hungry and releasing people from various kinds of prison. We'll see the kingdom sooner if we begin to eliminate the injustice that leads to hunger and if we start working to ensure that all children receive the love they need and deserve. That's going to mean changing how we live our lives.

We're often afraid of what that change is going to do to us. Jesus talked about war, earthquake, and famine—and change often feels like that. Yet I'm always amazed at the good deeds that erupt in the midst of those disasters. When there's a flood or a forest fire or an earthquake, people remember what's most important, and ultimately, it isn't the stuff in the safe-deposit box. It's the human connections, and the realization that we matter to one another, and that if we pull together this world can indeed be a far more divine place.

What part of our world needs change the most right now? We've been talking a lot about the need for health-care reform here in the United States. That has people riled up because they're afraid that it will cost them money or involve change in their own health-care options. Yet the reality is that if nothing changes, fewer and fewer people in this country will have access to adequate health care. The more people seek care in emergency rooms, the more expensive medical care becomes for all of us. Yes, there is a short-term cost, but the benefits are both practical and divine—a healthier economy if more are ready and able to work, and a healthier society when all are treated with dignity. Do we have the courage and hope to change?

More globally, we're talking about changes in environmental conditions, the warming of our planet, and the consequences of continuing with business as usual. Those climatic changes are already having significant consequences, most of them hardest on people with the least capacity to cope. Sea level is rising and already displacing the peoples of South Pacific islands. It's already harder to grow crops in an increasingly arid sub-Saharan Africa. If we're going to confront the changes in our global climate, we're going to have to change the way we live here at home—including kicking our addiction to carbon-based fuels. It's already possible—though more expensive—to produce all the power we need in this country with renewable energy—without the use of nuclear power. But it will take a common mind and the will to change. Some folks will think this change means the world is ending—and they're right, if we're talking about a world built on fossil fuels. God is already inviting us into a different future. The question is whether or not we're willing to look for hope in the midst of these cataclysmic changes.

Even the church is changing, and it always has been. The conversation Jesus has about the stones of the temple coming down is about a structural change: at the moment he spoke those words, religion as people in his world knew it was shifting, and both Christianity and modern Judaism were the result. We're working through another round of change right now. In The Episcopal Church lots of people still call the 1979 Book of Common Prayer that we use today "the new prayer book," but very few of us would go back to the old one, with its lofty but stilted language. Almost none of us would go back to the world of hats and white gloves and no girl acolytes.

Change is part of life, and it can feel like the world is coming to an end. In spite of our fear, we hope and pray for that change because we know that God has a better world in mind—that dream called the kingdom of God, or the commonweal of God. We can deal with our fear when we remember that death never has the last word, and that resurrection is already erupting in the face of death.

I saw a glimpse of the reign of God that Sunday of the loud Lord's Prayer. Joy and laughter were a sign of God's presence. So was my friend's willingness to have those two kids shout out their prayer as a remarkably creative upset to all the stuffy adults around him, including me. He had it exactly right—we should all be shouting, "YOUR KINGDOM COME."

Blessed, indeed, are the change makers.

For Reflection

What can you do to provoke love and good deeds, and the change that's necessary to make them happen? How loud can you pray?

Provoking Love

No one has ever seen God; if we love one another, God lives in us, and his love is perfected in us. By this we know that we abide in him and he in us, because he has given us of his Spirit.

—1 JOHN 4:11–13

I get to see some remarkable communities of faith in my travels, people of many different languages and tribes, cultures and traditions. Not too long ago, I worshiped with a Hmong congregation in Minnesota. Recently I was in Boston, where the cathedral provides space for a Chinese student congregation and a ministry that feeds the homeless—each community is cared for in loving ways. And one Sunday I was in Mobile, Alabama, where we baptized an eleven-year-old boy, the child of addicted parents, who came to church on his own, found a loving home and substitute family, and eventually insisted on being baptized. After the service we went to dedicate a Habitat for Humanity house for a Sudanese refugee family who have resettled there. All over The Episcopal Church—all over the country—there are communities telling good news and being good news to people who need to hear that they're loved, and who are offered that love in concrete ways. The people and communities who feed the hungry and house the homeless and welcome the hurting and heal the sick are doing that work because someone challenged them to love others the way they've been loved. Those people of faith are loving their neighbors because that's what Jesus did. They aren't loving their neighbors because somebody told them what wretched people they were. The Christians who show the world what love looks like don't do it out of fear. As Paul's letter to the Romans says, the spirit leads us into awareness that we are children of God—and it's not a spirit of fear, but of love (Romans 8:16). John's gospel is pretty blunt about it. The paraphrased version of the Bible called *The Message* puts it like this: "God didn't go to all the trouble of sending his Son merely to point an accusing finger, telling the world how bad it was. He came to help, to put the world right again" (John 3:16).[1] The gospel is about the good news of God's love. And when we really and truly know we are well loved, we begin to be able to respond in kind.

In 1928, the Episcopal bishop of Alabama heard that there were some Indians—as Native Americans were called at that time—living out in the woods northeast of Mobile. He sent a missionary out to see who was there. The missionary did indeed discover a band of Creek Indians, in a place called Poarch. Their ancestors had hidden themselves away during the great removal in the 1830s, when the United States government tried to eliminate all Native Americans in the southeast by sending them to Oklahoma. Most of the Creek people were driven out to endure that Trail of Tears, along with the Choctaw, Seminole, Chickasaw, and Cherokee.

The missionary who went out to Poarch discovered people who needed food and clothing and education during the Great Depression, and he helped mobilize the larger church to respond. He settled in and discovered a people who bathed in the creek every morning (which is where their English name comes from), and prayed to the Great Creator as they turned to face the four directions. As those Creek people learned about Jesus through the concrete experience of love, they also heard some parallels with their own experience of the Great Creator. They began to ask to be baptized. The missionary baptized many, in the same swimming hole where they had long said their morning prayers. And the missionary recorded all those baptisms, and the births and marriages and deaths in the community, and his successor continued to write down those names and dates.

In 1977 the Poarch Band of Creek Indians applied to the U.S. government for formal recognition, and in 1983 it was awarded, mostly as a result of all those parish records, substantiating relationships and an ongoing connection with the land in Poarch. The church also gave a piece of land to the tribe—seventeen acres that became the first part of the Poarch Creek reservation. Today about 1,700 members live on reservation lands, a checkerboard of about 450 acres in southern Alabama. They also have a casino that seems to be doing very well, and out of the proceeds the tribe provides health care, housing support, and scholarships for any member who wants to pursue vocational training or higher education.

Without the willingness of someone to go to rural Alabama eighty years ago, this group of people would by now almost certainly have lost its identity. I was in Poarch not too long ago, and it was immensely humbling to hear the elders speak of the work of this Episcopal church with such reverence and gratitude.

That reality of new and more abundant life is the result of somebody being willing to go and share the love that he already knew. That's what happens every time we baptize someone. We hear God saying to us what God said to Jesus at his baptism: "You are my beloved, and in you I am well pleased" (Matthew 3:17; my translation). Most of us are baptized as babies, but the rites of confirmation and reception are opportunities for Christian people to claim that belovedness in a conscious and public way—to claim God's love and commit to living in a way that shows and shares that love with the world. In The Episcopal Church, candidates for confirmation renew the five promises of baptism about how they will live in the world. Drawing from the Book of Common Prayer, they promise to:

1. Continue in the apostles' teaching and fellowship
2. Persevere in resisting evil

3. Proclaim the gospel "by word and example"
4. Seek and serve Jesus in everyone, "loving our neighbor as ourselves"
5. Strive for justice and peace

Baptism and the rites connected with it are what Jesus called being "born from above" and being "born of water and Spirit" (John 3:5–7). They are an invitation to see the kingdom of God, the world in which love is the way we relate to each other. Love as the way we relate to others is a reflection of the God we know as Trinity. It's a way of saying that God in God's own self is social, relational, and loving. When we show love to the world, we become the image of God, and the presence of God's love.

Recently, I heard some people talk about how they show love to the world. One young woman spoke about going to coastal Mississippi right after Katrina, and spending six months doing whatever she could to be useful—mucking out houses, organizing a big repository of canned food, hammering nails. Another fellow talked about the thirty years he spent working in a butcher shop, trying to evangelize his buddies. He said he finally learned that his job wasn't to get somebody to say a verbal formula about accepting Jesus as personal lord and savior, but to make a space that was safe enough for others to say what they really think and feel. A retired woman said that her way of being love in the world was to be mindful, to be aware of the person right in front of her, and the opportunities for hospitality and kindness. And the last one, a twenty-six-year-old woman, said that hers was to meet people at their deepest vulnerability—in her work as a home visitor for child protective services, in the Spanish worship service at her church, or among the spiritually hungry people she meets who are simply looking for a connection. Each one of those people was talking about being love in the world. That's what it means to live as a beloved child of God.

I saw a small example one morning when I was running along the river in Salem, Oregon. The riverwalk is paved with bricks that have donors' names etched on them, and with small decorative tiles made by children—surprising bits of color and creativity in the long stretches of paving. Both are small, sacramental signs that somebody loves you enough to make this a more beautiful place. Those bricks and tiles, and the ways we are present in this world, are all real, concrete evidence of the change God's love can make in the world—in our personal lives as well as in our communal lives.

For Reflection

How will you provoke love in this world?

Interrupting
Business as Usual

Then Jesus called the twelve together and gave them power and authority over all demons and to cure diseases, and he sent them out to proclaim the kingdom of God and to heal. He said to them, "Take nothing for your journey, no staff, nor bag, nor bread, nor money—not even an extra tunic. Whatever house you enter, stay there, and leave from there. Wherever they do not welcome you, as you are leaving that town shake the dust off your feet as a testimony against them." They departed and went through the villages, bringing the good news and curing diseases everywhere.

—LUKE 9:1–6

Shortly after I took office as The Episcopal Church's Presiding Bishop, somebody at the Church Center in New York mentioned a wild and crazy idea about sending fifty young adults out to prowl around New York City as urban missioners—people who might share their faith and transform the little communities in which they lived and moved and had their being. It was sort of like urban Christianity going viral.

Nobody has started any formal program yet, but recently I did meet a youth group from South Carolina who had come to New York on a pilgrimage and were doing just that. When I asked these kids from Holy Cross Church in Simpsonville what they were doing on their pilgrimage, they told me about stopping earnest and highly focused commuters with high fives, and the variety of reactions they received—almost all of them positive. They were actually surprised that these formal, black-clad New Yorkers would stop and engage them. They also told me about their plans for the following day— offering free hugs. I mused with them about how their interactions had changed people's lives, and later on I reflected about how their ministry of interruption is a lot like the work of the spirit in our own lives. A small dose of reconciliation, a brief invitation to see the world as more gracious than it seemed when you rolled out of bed at five o'clock with a two-hour commute in front of you and headed to a job that is as soulless and unsatisfying as yesterday and last month.

That's really what all mission is about—an interruption of the world's way of seeing reality as grim and pretty hopeless, of assuming that violence is just the way the world is, and anonymity is the best way to get along.

Mission is about co-creating a different reality. It's about partnering with God to insist that there is hope abundant for a world where people don't need to study military strategy any more because no one ignores hungry neighbors. When everyone has enough to eat, and the security in which to eat one's fill, no one will see a need to study war any more. Jesus insists that a world like that is possible— this world is ripe and ready for it. We just need to send out some more interrupters, some more harvesters, to remind everyone of the abundance around us. Yes, indeed, the kingdom of God has come near.

Abundance. When we see it, we don't resort to war. When we recognize the abundance in our own lives, we respond with open hands, so that all can enjoy that abundance. That's why Jesus insists that his disciples be satisfied with what they're served—it is enough and more than enough, if you don't see scarcity. It's manna, the bountiful gift of God that the Jews received when they were wandering in the desert on their long road to the promised land. And don't take your extra suitcase full of stuff, Jesus tells them, because the people you meet will share their own abundance with you— there *will* be enough.

Jesus has more counsel for his disciples: When you knock on a door and they let you in, announce peace and don't complain about the rain or the heat (I'm still working on that one). See the blessed welcome you are offered and offer healing in return—healing of the whole person. Even mainstream American medicine is beginning to appreciate that healing is far more than fixing a physical problem. You can do all the bypasses you want, but if the rest of life doesn't change, those arteries are going to be plugged up again in a few years. Even if a person gets a terminal diagnosis, healing is still possible—the kind of healing that comes with the presence of friends and relatives surrounding a dying person's bed, and the ultimate healing we know in God.

When Jesus insists that we heal one another, he means all those things and more. He means healing like the hard psychospiritual work adults have to wrestle with in order to heal the mistakes their well-meaning but imperfect parents made in raising them. He means the tough work of changing social systems toward justice for every human being, so that there are no more "accidents" of hunger. And he means healing our relationship with the rest of creation.

Jesus' mission is healing the whole world, and that mission needs all of us, and every partner we can find. Feeding the hungry and clothing the naked are the easy tasks. They only require that we discover our abundant gifts in those departments and the companionable space where our neighbors need those gifts. The healing that we who are over-endowed with food or clothing receive comes in discovering the companions we never knew—companions are literally those with whom we share bread. When God says in creation that it is not good for Adam (the earth creature) to be alone, it's a profoundly true indictment of the Western heresy that we can ever be complete, whole, or holy in isolation. We are meant for relationship, and we discover the healing of our own isolation in feeding our hungry neighbors and comforting the grieving.

Jesus shows us that reality over and over and over again. Even hanging on the cross, he reaches out to his fellow criminals, building connections and healing relationships: "Today you will be with me in paradise," he says to the thief who is hanging at his side (Luke 23:43). Remember that his very first claim about his mission foreshadowed the healing that would be an integral part of it. In his "inaugural address," speaking in his hometown synagogue, he proclaimed: "The Spirit of the Lord is upon me, because he has anointed me to bring good news to the poor. He has sent me to proclaim release to the captives" and he finishes by saying, "Today this scripture has been fulfilled in your hearing" (Luke 4:18–21).

Throughout the country, communities of faith are deeply invested in healing—feeding the hungry, helping the homeless find a way to greater stability, drilling water wells in the developing world, helping prostitutes find a healed life. They are working at expanding relationships in redemptive directions between human beings and the rest of God's creation—and between people of different races. The work that people of faith do, of course, won't be finished until we can see the imprint of the creator in each part of creation, and not just the image of the divine in human form. God has created all that is, and all of it carries an echo of the holy. Creation is not simply a credit card for our latest shopping spree—which is how much of the Western world still sees it. Creation is not a commodity for our use alone. Creation is an abundant gift of God, meant to bless all, not merely a few.

The mission work, the harvest work, is largely about interrupting our old familiar ways of seeing—or letting God interrupt us—by discovering abundance where we thought there was only scarcity, discovering healing in the midst of illness, discovering a friend in the stranger. Those kids with their high fives and free hugs are on to something.

For Reflection

What kind of interruptions will you go out there and cause?

Mission Possible

These twelve Jesus sent out with the following instructions: "Go nowhere among the Gentiles, and enter no town of the Samaritans, but go rather to the lost sheep of the house of Israel. As you go, proclaim the good news, 'The kingdom of heaven has come near.' Cure the sick, raise the dead, cleanse the lepers, cast out demons. You received without payment; give without payment. Take no gold, or silver, or copper in your belts, no bag for your journey, or two tunics, or sandals, or a staff; for laborers deserve their food. Whatever town or village you enter, find out who in it is worthy, and stay there until you leave. As you enter the house, greet it. If the house is worthy, let your peace come upon it; but if it is not worthy, let your peace return to you."

—MATTHEW 10:5–13

When we go out into the world to spread the gospel, Jesus tells us a little something about what to put in our suitcase: "no purse, no bag, no sandals" (Luke 10:4). We're supposed to depend on God, in the hospitality of those we meet. Despite our need to be in control, and to be prepared for any possible turn of events, the gospel remains, to challenge us all: travel light.

Episcopalians are like Boy Scouts—we like to be ready, with prayer book, hymnal, and bulletin in hand, and a Swiss army knife in our back pocket to open the wine bottle. When nineteenth-century missionaries went out to foreign lands, they took everything they thought they were going to need—they often shipped their goods out in a coffin, not expecting to return—and though they may have cut some ties with home, they still took plenty of cultural baggage with them.

Episcopalians have quite a love for order, and every three years we meet at our General Convention to process and organize and structure our lives together. The challenge is that structure or culture can become an idol, an image of our lust for control. Jesus isn't interested in taking extra rations or all the comforts of home or making hotel reservations for every stop on the journey.

Jesus simply sends the disciples out and tells them to travel light and expect hospitality. Their job is to share their hosts' tables, heal wherever they go, and announce peace and the reign of God.

Travel light. As we journey through life, is our goal how much stuff we can accumulate? Or is the journey itself our goal? We can load up on books and gadgets and nice new shoes, but are we open enough to receive the surprising gifts that are offered to us every day—the guy who gives us a seat on the bus or the train, the smile we get from the barista who serves us our morning cup of coffee, the hundred and one gifts of hospitality that we don't always seem to notice. What do we need to put down or leave behind in order to receive those unexpected gifts? Traveling light has a great deal to do with expecting to find the presence of God, gracious welcome, hospitality, and the image of God in everyone we meet.

Jesus sends those seventy disciples out to interrupt the day-to-day lives of their hosts, to heal people who probably didn't expect any healing, and to offer the shocking news that the reign of God is already here. If those seventy don't receive peace from the folks they encounter, Jesus tells them, they're just supposed to move on—there are plenty of other opportunities to offer the peace of God. Those seventy just *go*, and they go ahead of Jesus. They're not following him around—they're the advance team, the roadies.

Are we ready to be sent? Are we ready to go ahead of Jesus, to prepare the way? The advance team is expected to find evidence of the presence of God before they begin to talk about Jesus or the reign of God. Paul of Tarsus—St. Paul, the apostle to the Gentiles and the writer of a number of letters to early Christian communities—went on a number of mission journeys and encouraged others to follow his example: "You are no longer strangers and aliens," says the Letter to the Ephesians, "but fellow citizens with God's people and members of God's household" (Ephesians 2:19; my translation). We aren't strangers and aliens any more, he reminds us, and it's the task of missionaries—that's us—to discover and proclaim that good news of loving welcome in Jesus.

Paul was a master at expecting hospitality, even in a hostile jail. Roland Allen, mentioned earlier, was also a light traveler. His work took root, and grew and flourished, often quietly, until the church in China today has become what he suggested: self-sustaining, self-propagating, and self-governing. It has even taken that as part of its name—the Three-Self Patriotic Movement. Individual congregations may have liturgical and theological leanings that we might recognize as Anglican or Methodist or Pentecostal, but the church as a whole has traveled lightly enough to take root in a different culture and context and become a new and different expression of the body of Christ.

How much of a burden is culture or structure? Can we receive what we are offered, can we announce peace or provide healing, with a bit less of the culture and structure we've come to rely on? The church cannot be all things to all people, except through all its members. Those human faces become the living image of God to a hurting world, pronouncing peace, offering healing, and working for unity. This body can only do that work through those who are sent out, having been fed for service, now fit for mission. Traveling light includes the willingness to share ministry and discover the gifts of others. And it means being a little bit less attached to whatever culture we hold most dear—church structure, the idiosyncrasies of our congregation or denomination—in order to focus more clearly on mission, just as Jesus instructed those first seventy missioners to do.

Our work on behalf of others, and our generosity, are sacraments of traveling light. When we hold something lightly, we're much more able to offer it, like sharing peace—if it's here, great, if not, let it go and move on. In The Episcopal Church, the United Thank Offering is a sacramental sign of our inward gratitude for each gift we receive, turned to outward and visible mission. This sign goes to help people in places from Puerto Rico and Tanzania, to Liberia and Alaska. *Claro que el reino de Dios esta muy cerca.* Clearly the kingdom of God is close at hand.

All over The Episcopal Church, and well beyond, God's people are feeding, healing, and announcing peace and the reign of God. The First Nations Kitchen in Minneapolis welcomes Native Americans to a meal of traditional and healthy foods within a healing community. Teaching ministries heal deprivation and hopelessness in Boston, Taiwan, and Quito. Physical illness is being healed in the clinics of the Diocese of the Dominican Republic and the Diocese of Honduras, in the nursing school of Haiti, through elder care in Native communities in Alabama and Minnesota, in hospitals in Oregon, Texas, Long Island, and Jerusalem. Camping ministries in the Central Gulf Coast, west Texas, California, and Mississippi teach children and adults to travel light and eat whatever is set before them.

As Christians, mission is our life, and it is a life spent on the road, traveling light, anticipating hospitality, and sharing everything that we have.

Most of us aren't going very far out into the world. Not many of us are called to be missionaries in far-off places. But we can announce peace at the office or the mall or the classroom. We can live out our mission of healing wherever our lives happen to take us.

As we go about our ordinary business, what welcome will we offer, and what will we receive? We're sent to be an interrupter of the world's business as usual—and we're sent to *be* interrupted. The reign of God, the commonwealth of God, is breaking in, whether we're ready or not. Our job is just what Jesus tells his disciples in the gospel: to go out there, engage the world, and become sacrament— an outward sign of the reign of God.

For Reflection

Where will you announce peace? How will you offer healing?

Ubuntu

I will take you from the nations, and gather you from all the countries, and bring you into your own land. I will sprinkle clean water upon you, and you shall be clean from all your uncleannesses, and from all your idols I will cleanse you. A new heart I will give you, and a new spirit I will put within you; and I will remove from your body the heart of stone and give you a heart of flesh. I will put my spirit within you, and make you follow my statutes and be careful to observe my ordinances. Then you shall live in the land that I gave to your ancestors; and you shall be my people, and I will be your God. I will save you from all your uncleannesses, and I will summon the grain and make it abundant and lay no famine upon you. I will make the fruit of the tree and the produce of the field abundant, so that you may never again suffer the disgrace of famine among the nations.

—EZEKIEL 36:24–30

Not too many years ago, I had the great privilege to join in the consecration of a new bishop, who told an amazing story about the journey that had brought her to that place on a cold night in Seattle. At the end of the service, Victor Rivera, the retired bishop of San Joaquin, California, wrapped the new bishop—his daughter Nedi—in his own cope, the long, capelike garment worn by bishops. The story is all the more remarkable because, while he was bishop in San Joaquin, and for many years afterward, he had insisted that women should not be ordained as priests or bishops. He didn't attend Nedi's ordination as a priest, and he had never received communion from her, over the more than twenty-five years she served as priest. I asked Nedi later how her father had come to change his mind. Her response: "He didn't change his mind; he changed his heart."

When the Hebrew prophet Ezekiel says, "A new heart I will give you, and a new spirit I will put within you; and I will remove from your body the heart of stone and give you a heart of flesh" (Ezekiel 36:26), he is talking about a changed heart, but in an even more radical sense he means a heart transplant. Ezekiel is speaking to the disheartened Jewish people, exiled in Babylon in the sixth century BCE, yearning for home, aching to be reconciled, impatient to end their depressed and heartsick state.

Heart transplants are at least possible in this era of human history—brain transplants aren't yet—but Ezekiel is also talking about a brain transplant. His people understood the heart not as the seat of emotion but as the seat of decision making, the critical faculty of judgment.

Ezekiel says the body will be disinfected: "I will sprinkle clean water upon you, and you shall be clean" (Ezekiel 36:25). Then comes the surgery: "A new heart I will give you, and a new spirit" (Ezekiel 36:26). This is about a new way of understanding and acting. It is about new life that comes from living in a new way.

Ezekiel goes on to report God's word about the consequences of this new heart: abundant harvests and freedom from famine. This abundance, the prophet insists, will prompt the people to repentance for their misdeeds. Their towns will be repopulated, and the desolate land will flourish again. God's garden, Eden, will be recreated (Ezekiel 36:29–35).

A new heart results in renewed creation—that's the reconciling mission we Christians are so fond of talking about. We receive this new heart from Jesus, an organ donor who has given his life that all might indeed have more abundant life.

Hearts renewed stay that way, living flesh that doesn't harden into stone, when they continue to share that new life; the exercise of pumping, after all, keeps a heart healthy. Ezekiel's hearers need a heart transplant because they've forgotten that God is the source of their life and blessing—they've turned inward, becoming small and fearful. Their new life will flourish as the people receive the moist breath of a life-giving God, as they take in hope and possibility and the creative spirit of God, even in the face of crisis.

The Episcopal Church in the Philippines offers a remarkable example of what a healthy and life-sustaining heart looks like. The heart transplant began in 1898, with services held by chaplains of the occupying U.S. Army (during the American occupation of the Philippines that led to that country's struggle for independence). Though we would probably choose a different avenue, the miracle of new life happens even in war, and even in the midst of colonial structures. In 1901, The Episcopal Church's General Convention established the Missionary District of the Philippines and elected Charles Henry Brent as missionary bishop. The first Filipino clergy were ordained, and the missionary district became a diocese in 1937. By 1971, there were three dioceses and indigenous bishops in each. In 1990, the Episcopal Church in the Philippines became an autonomous province of the Anglican Communion, the worldwide association of churches that have their roots in the Church of England. A covenant relationship with The Episcopal Church continues to this day, and the Episcopal Church in the Philippines achieved financial independence in late 2007. Philippine Prime Bishop Edward Malecdan recently presented a significant financial gift to The Episcopal Church in gratitude for our continuing relationship, as a sign of the strong and growing heart of the church in the Philippines, eager to reach out to others in love. It is a sacrificial gift, and it will bring more abundant life to both donor and recipient.

The heart of the Philippine church began in the missionary heart of The Episcopal Church, as the heart of The Episcopal Church has its origins in missionary hearts in England, and going back over many centuries to the sacred heart of Jesus in whom we all find our home.

That transplanted or expanded heart has much to do with *ubuntu*—an African concept of personhood in which each person's identity is understood to be formed interdependently with all the other members of the community. *Ubuntu* is a recognition that the one body of Christ—all who believe in Jesus—has many parts, each essential to the functioning and flourishing of the whole, and no one part can be the whole. It is a deep and abiding acknowledgment that together we are whole, that we cannot be whole otherwise. When the parts of the body of Christ are working together, they discover both their gifts and their limitations. The little toe plays an important role in balance, but it can't smell, even if it is occasionally odorous. The elbow can't run, even though the energy it gives to a pumping arm can add stability and power to the whole body in a sprint.

The Episcopal Church in the Philippines can't serve as the primary church in Haiti, nor can The Episcopal Church still be the primary gospeller in the Philippines. Yet the full communion of partnership among all of our related Anglican and Episcopal churches enriches us all.

The first missionary bishop in the Philippines evidently understood this. He insisted that he wouldn't "found an altar against an altar." He wouldn't, he insisted, start Episcopal churches with the goal of converting Roman Catholics. He saw the mission of that nascent church as evangelical responsibility for English-speaking expatriates, and for the urban Chinese population, but more especially for the unevangelized peoples of the Philippine Islands. The strength of the Philippine church today largely comes from the indigenous people of the mountains and the lowlands, where Episcopal missionaries first took the gospel. Bishop Brent wouldn't let the missioners stay in the cities; he believed that those cities already had most of the altars they needed. He went looking for people who were open to being born again, from above. He went looking for people who, like the Jews in Ezekiel's day, were open to receiving a new heart and a new spirit.

That is still our mission work—taking good news and rebirth and offering heart transplants to those who are languishing. The heart of Christian communities will slowly turn to stone if we think our primary mission work is to those already in the pews inside our beautiful churches, or to those at other altars. We are in cardiac crisis if we think we can close the doors, swing our incense, and sing our hymns, and all will be right with the world. The heart of the church is mission—domestic and foreign mission, in partnership with anyone who shares that passion.

Jesus has already given his followers a new heart. Every time we gather—to worship, to pray, to work together for others—the Spirit offers a pacemaker jolt to tweak the rhythm of our hearts. The challenge is to recognize and receive that renewed life, to let that heart muscle respond with a strengthened beat, sending more life out into the world.

Eight centuries before Jesus, the prophet Ezekiel promised his listeners full larders and planted fields and repopulated cities. When they'd received all these promises, they responded with repentance, with *metanoia*, or change. They got a new mind—and a new heart. Once people recognize the overflowing abundance they've been given, they begin to reject the hardness of their hearts, and they experience new life. The abundant life we've been promised becomes a reality, and when we notice, we begin to accept the transplant. We will find more abundant life only in being poured out in giving life to the world.

So, how will this heart push more lifeblood out into a languishing world? Listen for the heartbeat. The heartbeat of this body of the church can and does echo the heartbeat of God—mission, mission, mission. When our hearts have been renewed, we respond in mission, being sent out to share God's abundance with others. For Christians, this is always true: We are inseparably bound together. Expressed in the language of *ubuntu*: I am because we are.

For Reflection

Where have you encountered *ubuntu* in your own life?

Part Three

Connecting with Creation

From the very beginning of creation—in the first chapter of the first book of the Hebrew Bible—God proclaimed that it was good. Our responsibility as people of faith is to be good and care-full stewards of the abundant gifts of creation. That means asking hard questions about the food we eat, the cars we drive, the houses we build—and recognizing that we are deeply connected to all that is.

God on the Gulf Coast

So God created the great sea monsters and every living creature that moves, of every kind, with which the waters swarm, and every winged bird of every kind. And God saw that it was good. God blessed them, saying, "Be fruitful and multiply and fill the waters in the seas, and let birds multiply on the earth."

—GENESIS 1:21–22

The original peoples of the North American continent understand that we are all connected, and that harm to one part of the sacred circle of life harms the whole. Scientists, both the ecological and physical sorts, know the same reality, although they express it in different terms. The Abrahamic faith traditions—Judaism, Christianity, and Islam—which all claim a common spiritual ancestor in Abraham, also charge human beings with care for the whole of creation, because it is God's good gift to humanity. Another way of saying this is that we are all connected and there is no escape; our common future depends on how we care for the rest of the natural world, not just the square feet of soil we may call our own. We breathe the same air, our food comes from the same ground and seas, and the water we have to share cycles through the same airshed, watershed, and terra firma.

The still-unfolding oil spill disaster in the Gulf of Mexico, which began on April 20, 2010, is good evidence of the interconnectedness of the whole. The disaster has its origins in our nation's addiction to oil, uninhibited growth, and consumerism, as well as old-fashioned greed and what the Christian tradition calls hubris and idolatry. Our collective sins are being visited on those who have had no part in them: birds, marine mammals, the tiny plants and animals that constitute the base of the vast food chain in the Gulf, and on which a major part of the seafood production of the United States depends. Our sins are being visited on the fishers of southern Louisiana, Mississippi, Alabama, and Florida, who seek to feed their families with the proceeds of what they catch each day. Our sins will expose New Orleans and other coastal cities to the increased likelihood of devastating floods, as the marshes that constitute the shrinking margin of storm protection continue to disappear, fouled and killed by oil.

The oil that vented from the sea floor for eighty-seven days has spread through hundreds of cubic miles of ocean, poisoning creatures of all sizes and forms, from birds, turtles, and whales to the shrimp, fish, oysters, and crabs that human beings so value, and the plankton, whose life supports the whole biological system—the very kind of creatures whose dead and decomposed tissues began the process of producing that oil so many millions of years ago.

We know, at least intellectually, that oil is a limited resource, yet we continue to extract and use it at increasing rates and with apparently decreasing care. The great scandal of this disaster is the one related to all kinds of "commons," resources held by the whole community. Like tropical forests in Madagascar and Brazil, and the gold and silver deposits of the American West, "commons" have in human history too often been greedily exploited by a few, with the aftermath left for others to deal with, or suffer with.

Yet the reality is that this disaster just may show us as a nation how interconnected we really are. The waste of this oil—both its unusability and the mess it is making—will be visited on all of us, for years and even generations to come. The hydrocarbons in those coastal marshes and at the base of the food chain leading to marketable seafood resources will taint us all, eventually. That oil has already begun to frighten away vacationers, who form the economic base for countless coastal communities, whose livelihoods contribute to the economic health of this nation. The workers in those communities, even when they have employment, are some of the poorest among us. That oil will move beyond the immediate environs of a broken wellhead, spreading around the coasts of Florida and northward along the east coast of the United States. That oil will foul the coastal marshes that also constitute a major nursery for coastal fauna, again a vital part of the food chain. That oil will further stress and poison the coral reefs of Florida, already much endangered from warming and ocean acidification. Those reefs have historically provided significant storm protection to the coastal communities behind them.

The chemical dispersants that are being so wantonly deployed to break up the oil will have consequences we're not yet cognizant of, and the experience of gold and silver mining in the West is instructive. The methods used in those old mining operations liberated plenty of arsenic, mercury, and other heavy metals, and left cyanide and acids, all of which have significant health effects on those who live, many years later, in the immediate area of mines and tailings, as well as those who use water downstream and breathe downwind air.

There is no place to go "away" from these consequences; there is no ultimate escape on this planet. The effects at a distance may seem minor or tolerable, but the cumulative effect is not. We are all connected, we will all suffer the consequences of this tragic disaster in the Gulf, and we must wake up and put a stop to the kind of robber baron behavior we supposedly regulated out of existence a hundred years ago. Our lives, and the liveliness of the entire planet, depend on it.

For Reflection

Consider the ways the Gulf oil spill has made you aware of the interconnections of humanity and the rest of creation.

Science and Faith

No man is an island, entire of itself; every man is a piece of the continent, a part of the main. If a clod be washed away by the sea, Europe is the less, as well as if promontory were, as well as if a manor of thy friend's or of thine own were. Any man's death diminishes me, because I am involved in mankind; and therefore never send to know for whom the bell tolls; it tolls for thee.

—JOHN DONNE, MEDITATION 17,
DEVOTIONS UPON EMERGENT OCCASIONS

Before I became a priest, I was a scientist who focused on the study of the oceans. My research started with near-shore marine communities, describing the species diversity and ecological structure. It moved later to looking at the ways that human intervention, in the form of harbor dredging, changed the structure and dynamics of similar marine communities. It went on from there to look at very large-scale oceanic systems and the ways in which squid and octopus populations shifted with water mass characteristics. And along the way, I dabbled in evolutionary theory and fisheries management.

When I tried to describe my work to laypeople, they would listen with varying degrees of interest, but were usually too polite to ask the question I think most of them were itching to ask: "What difference does that make for me? How will knowing more about mid-ocean populations of squid and octopus make my life better?" Or perhaps they would have liked to ask: "What impact will your work have on the larger human community?"

Most people, after all, are interested in the connection with their own lives, and all scientists have some responsibility to translate their research into those terms. That's the premise under which publishing the results of our research operates. It's not just a hazing mechanism for getting tenure or the next grant—it's about sharing what we've learned with others and learning about the world together.

This assumption about communicating the results of our work is built into the system of science. Scientists have to tell others what they're doing, beginning with their immediate colleagues and expanding into the larger society. That expectation is a recognition of our interconnection with scientific peers, with the larger institutions that support scientific research, and with the larger human community.

Out of this initial responsibility to communicate the results of research emerges a wider ethical responsibility. The duty to communicate assumes truthful communication. Scientists can't shade or misrepresent the results of their research, nor should they publish work that's trivial or meaningless. One of the most painful issues in the scientific community involves the exposure of researchers who falsify data or misreport their results. The scientific community cannot tolerate untruth, and that community's response is usually swift and final. It is a reflection of most scientists' awareness of the implied trust placed in them.

That implied trust extends to the need not only for truthful reporting of research results, but the expectation that scientists will warn the larger community about the hazards of particular research directions. There are many examples, from expectations about informed consent by human research subjects, to the need for accelerated warnings when research reveals unanticipated implications. If a soils study shows that an earthen dam is inherently unstable, does an ethical investigator wait to say something until her paper is published? The people who live downstream certainly hope not—and they have a reasonable expectation to be informed, for their own safety and that of the larger community.

One of the social or ethical responsibilities of scientists is generally understood to include minimizing harm. There is often an assumption that the calculus of potential harms is balanced in favor of human well-being. It should be immediately evident that it's impossible to avoid any human harm, though most ethical researchers seek to minimize it. From the hazards of life as a sea-going oceanographer, to the risks of working with specimens preserved in formalin, to the social hazards of excessive focus on the academy rather than a person's own family or his or her physical condition, research has human costs. There are larger costs to the human community when research privileges certain questions, such as the long-term focus on cardiac disease that for years only studied men, or the difficulty in finding research support for diseases that affect relatively few.

The scientific community has a duty to the larger society that involves asking the more challenging questions about its own functioning. Some within the community have always had the courage and chutzpah to ask those questions. One Polish scientist reluctantly agreed to work on the Manhattan Project, which developed the atom bomb for the Allied nations during World War II, and continued to contribute vigorously, until he became convinced that the opposing forces, the Axis nations, would not develop an atomic weapon of their own before the war ended. At that point—in 1944—his conscience led him to leave the project. Even today, other scientists continue to ask if accepting any funding from military sources is justified, on the theory that ultimately, that kind of work contributes to violence against other human beings.

Archaeologists, whose work often destroys the sites on which they work, are increasingly electing to excavate only a portion of new sites, assuming that their future colleagues will have less invasive techniques.

Social and neurological scientists ask about the use of deception with human subjects. Double-blind studies, for instance, while not intentionally misleading, do not provide subjects with all possible knowledge about their participation—they don't know if they will receive a placebo or a potentially effective drug. Today, research protocols usually stop a study when the data reveal either significant potential benefit or harm. The scientific community routinely makes judgments in these matters based on a calculus of individual rights versus benefit to the larger society, and assumes that the autonomy of the patient, the ability to elect participation or not, relieves most of the tension. Yet scientists are still left with many questions about consent, and whether it really is adequately informed.

Some portions of the scientific community have begun to ask challenging questions about the effects of research on nonhuman species, and where the balance should lie in terms of potential benefit and harm. Is harm to nonhuman creatures acceptable in all circumstances? Is it only acceptable if it results in significant human benefit? Or is harming nonhuman creatures not acceptable in any case at all?

The larger question is whether the nonhuman part of the world has intrinsic value, or only has value as it provides resources for human beings. Is it to be treated only as commodity? The voices being raised now cross a fairly broad spectrum, from the Animal Liberation Front to conservative and traditional people of faith, who are willing to see evidence of the divine in creatures other than human.

In this era of human history, it is now imperative that scientists be deeply involved in questions about the long-term viability of the planetary ecosystem. The scientific community has been effective in raising the level of concern about the effects of fossil fuel use, and proposing alternative fuel use and conservation scenarios. The broader responsibility has to do with urgency, which parts of the ecosystem are likely to bear the burden, and how to ameliorate both the damage and the burden. One significant question might be whether or not it is ethical to continue major exploratory efforts for fossil fuels without concomitant research on remediation, reducing the environmental burdens of carbon-based fuel use, and/or increasing investment in green energy. This is a question that has become even more important, and more urgent, in the wake of the Gulf oil spill.

The scientific community has at least the theoretical ability to have honest conversations about the pros and cons and limitations of different directions of research and potential consequences, based on objective evidence. That kind of conversation can be a gift to most human communities. Facilitating that kind of conversation is part of the overarching duty of the scientific community to communicate. It seems especially important in matters where there is a great deal of emotional freight or uncertainty, or when the consequences of particular actions or inaction are of major significance.

Individual scientists may reach different conclusions about the ethics of particular kinds of research, and in retrospect some of the ignorance of harm—and attitudinal certainty about its absence—can be starkly shocking. Marie Curie died of radiation-related disease after decades of remarkable discoveries. In the 1960s and '70s there was immense investment in research on possible peaceful uses of nuclear explosions for excavation and earth-moving projects—with little positive result, beyond the conclusion that there are less expensive and less destructive ways to accomplish the same ends. Today there is a similar uncertainty or varied opinion about biofuel crops, stem-cell research, and human cloning. The very passion that's expressed in these discussions is an indication of the greater need for the scientific community's engagement with the larger society. None of us can hide behind the technical work and leave the ethical work to other experts—it requires a partnership. No reasonable conclusion can be reached without voices who will speak for the marginalized—those without advocates—including the very young and very old and the disabled, as well as nonhuman species, larger ecosystems, and the earth itself.

The scientific community, like most faith communities, understands the nature of interconnection. Extinction of one species in an ecosystem has effects far beyond the local. The spin of a particle in space A is linked to its partner's spin in space B. At the level of quantum physics, there is good evidence that consequences extend beyond the "local" and that measurements in one space result in knowing what the state of a particle is in another space. Acidification of the oceans is already threatening a number of ecosystems and fisheries. While the pH of the ocean directly affects the ability of some shelled organisms to survive, those same organisms' health affects other species. Native peoples on the North Slope of Alaska find it harder to maintain their ancient life-ways and culture as the polar ice cover thins and permafrost melts. The caribou on which the Gwich'in people depend cannot migrate to and from their habitual grazing and calving grounds when the permafrost melts. The people who depend on those herds are losing their ability to survive in traditional ways. This interconnectedness exists in society as well as in our relationship to the natural world. The recent controversy about cancer screening guidelines presents a stark contrast between patients' rights to make their own treatment decisions and the cost of useless treatment to the larger society.

We are all connected, and scientists have a responsibility to tell the truth they know and invite others into challenging conversations about what nobody knows. We fail our vocation as members of a larger system—academic, human, global, and yes, spiritual—when we're unwilling to tell the truth. That truth telling can be an invitation to greater awe and wonder as well as a sense of human limits in the face of the divine.

For Reflection

How are you interconnected with the world around you? Why does it matter?

The Ecology of Faith

Blessed are those who trust in the Lord,
whose trust is the Lord.
They shall be like a tree planted by water,
sending out its roots by the stream.
It shall not fear when heat comes,
and its leaves shall stay green;
in the year of drought it is not anxious,
and it does not cease to bear fruit.
—JEREMIAH 17:7–8

Have you ever thought about what it would be like to be a plant? Consider one of those great redwoods growing along the northern California coast. How do they get to be nearly four hundred feet tall? The sheer effort that's required to pump water from the roots up to the top of a tree like that is just about physically impossible. Those trees can get so big only because they've figured out some creative ways to get a little more water, such as harvesting the fog that condenses on their branches way up there. The very biggest ones grow alongside year-round streams in the fog zone, thriving only because of their constant access to water.

Other kinds of plants have solved the water problem in equally creative ways. The barrel cactuses of the American Southwest can actually expand their tissues, in big pleats, when there's water available. Those pleats contract slowly over months and even years between rainstorms, providing a constant supply of water.

Bromeliads—plants such as Spanish moss and pineapples—can grow high in the air on the branches of other plants, or in desert climates, because they have adapted to capture water and nutrients in little bowls made of their own leaves, or through special structures in their leaves. Their roots are pretty much used only to hold them in place.

Others, including the pitcher plants in a few places on the Pacific coast, have responded to the challenge of growing in swamps, with their feet in places that often lack nutrients, by getting nitrogen from attracting and trapping insects and slowly digesting them.

Each and every living being has to figure out how to get the stuff of life, in easy circumstances and hard ones. The Hebrew prophet Jeremiah reminds the people of Israel that their life comes from putting down roots close by streams of living water (Jeremiah 17:8). It's an image that Jesus takes up later, telling the woman he meets at the well that he can connect her with that living water (John 4:6–15).

For Christians, that's what baptism is all about—getting connected to the water of life. In the early church, and still in some places today, it actually means getting your feet wet, and all the rest of you, being submerged in that living water. I have a good friend who tells of her own baptism at age nine in a Baptist church. She says that the pastor pushed her down hard into a deep pool of water, and she went down, down, down, until her feet finally touched the bottom and she pushed off, desperately seeking air at the top of the pool. Her gasping first breath was a reminder of her need for connection with the source of all life.

Christians are baptized into Jesus' death, which is what that near-drowning is all about, and into his resurrection, that rich and deep breath of life. But we are also baptized into his baptism, which is something we may not think about very often. The water of baptism is a connection with the Jordan River, and Jesus' own recognition of his connection to the source of living water. When Jesus comes up out of the water, the heavenly voice reminds him, "You are my beloved, and in you I am well pleased" (Luke 3:22; my translation). God says the same to each one of us.

That is our living water, our connection to the wellspring of love and life. When we know ourselves beloved, we discover that life is not a zero-sum game. Like Jesus' disciples jockeying for position, we can learn that competition isn't really necessary. The reality is that each one of us is God's best-beloved, infinitely valued for who we are, and not for what we do or make or earn. In fact, we can't earn that infinitely positive regard. We can only let our roots keep growing deeper into that source of life.

Living beings that have their roots well supplied with water bear abundant fruit. In the Christian ecosystem, the fruit we bear looks like service, healing, feeding, and caring for the neighbor who is also God's best-beloved. There's a deep connection between being well watered and caring for our neighbors.

I read a remarkable little article recently that talked about how altruistic behavior might evolve. Sarah Coakley is a British theologian who thinks about such things, and she points out that the cooperative behavior in less complex creatures such as bacteria is a prelude to the kind of human behavior that's usually called sacrificial.[1]

How do we move from competition to cooperation to sacrifice? It happens in creatures that came along before we did—it's not simply the product of so-called "higher consciousness." Even plants such as redwoods have evolved in cooperative ways. Those great big trees usually bear other plants, such as ferns and even small trees, high in their branches. For a long time, people thought they were just parasites, costing the redwoods something but offering nothing in return. It turns out that those epiphytes—plants that grow on other plants—aren't just freeloaders. They're providing more surface area to catch fog, and they actually produce nutrients that the redwood can use. It's a cooperative system, and each member is significant.

The human challenge is to learn to choose this kind of behavior—the sacrificial or making-holy behavior that's involved in loving others. Some people think sacrifice is just giving up goodies so that somebody else can have them all. God's economy, the divine ecology, is a whole lot more complex and mysterious than that.

In the gospel story, two of Jesus' disciples, James and John, are out to get the seats of honor, competing with the other disciples for the only "goodies" they can think of—a place at Jesus' right hand when they join him in heaven (Mark 10:34–45). It's classically competitive behavior: "Let me get mine before anybody else can steal it." But Jesus calls James and John back to the holy act that seeks the well-being of others in addition to their own and reminds them that friends of Jesus are here to serve, to offer themselves on behalf of others. That's what we as Christians are baptized into; that's the water we drink in with our roots. And before long we discover that what seems to be giving up actually produces more—we discover our lives by giving them away. That is "holy-making," or *sacrificium*, which is the root of the word *sacrifice*.

This is the sacrificial behavior that Jesus models for us. The one who is best-beloved loves others in the way that God loves, seeking the utmost well-being of others, and offering self for others.

Living water makes us holy, and actually makes more of us and more life. When our roots extend deep into that source of life, we discover far more abundant life than we could ever have imagined—all around us. Consider the following examples:

A fourteen-year-old girl in Bethlehem, Pennsylvania, started an animal food bank when she realized that many of the people being fed by her church's food bank also had pets, and if their human beings were hungry, then the pets likely were as well. Today that animal food bank feeds about a thousand creatures a month.

In Kansas City, the stream that flows through the middle of town shelters lots of homeless people under the bridges that cross it. A big Episcopal congregation in Mission, Kansas, began to take those people meals on Thanksgiving and Christmas, when the soup kitchens were closed. When they asked these folks with nowhere to lay their heads what they most wanted, the response was, "We need someone to pray with us." Now the members of that congregation are working to start a worship service for people who feel uncomfortable inside church. So far, they haven't found a vacant lot or a park where they'd be welcome to worship, but I think these resourceful Christians will figure out how to convince the mayor he needs to help. And in doing so, they will help him make holy, too.

The water in Sioux Falls, South Dakota, has connected Episcopalians with Sudanese refugees resettled there, people who've been Anglicans since they can remember. Together they're building schools and churches and digging wells in the villages in Sudan.

In Atlanta, the water is flowing out into an arts program for the mentally disabled, a program that outgrew the local Episcopal church and is now sheltered in a Baptist one.

It's amazing what that water can do when your roots drink deep. In God's ecology, our roots are all entangled and we are connected to one another and to all of creation. God speaks to us not only through other human beings but also through the rest of creation.

For Reflection

Think about the ways that nature teaches us about the divine. How are creation and God connected?

Good Shepherd

I am the good shepherd; I know my sheep and my sheep know me—just as the Father knows me and I know the Father—and I lay down my life for the sheep.

—JOHN 10:14–15 (NIV)

Who calls us by name? Loved ones, friends, coworkers, and probably the receptionist at the doctor's office. Most of us guard our names from strangers, in the same way that we guard our passports or ID cards. There's an intimacy that comes with being known by name that even the raging extroverts among us don't grant to everyone. Notice how many online comments are made under pseudonyms—those who make attacks or less than kind observations prefer to do it anonymously.

Our culture still maintains some reluctance to address strangers by their first name. To know and use someone's name, particularly a first name, is to have some claim on that person, some expectation of intimacy and access. We call people by name at important points in their Christian lives—when they're baptized, married, and buried, and when we pray for them in specific ways. Some congregations—usually smaller ones—make a point of naming people at communion. Jesus is named at his baptism, when the spirit calls him "my beloved, in whom I am well pleased." That language is also the way God addresses us: "You are my beloved, and in you I am well pleased." And that's the kind of relationship Jesus as good shepherd is claiming with his sheep: "My sheep hear my voice. I know them, and they follow me."

Any kind of leader-follower relationship depends on some degree of knowing and being known, almost always by name. The military formalizes address by title and last name—so do schools and our legislative bodies. Both political campaigns and community organizing depend on knowing the people of a community and their desires. When a leader can speak to the inner hurts, joys, sorrows, or hopes of others, that leader begins to become effective.

We look for different kinds of leaders at different points in our lives. When we're anxious, we seem to be more interested in an enforcer—a great big bulldog, nipping at heels, to make us or others get in line. That seems to be what's pushing a lot of the polarizing political rhetoric these days—life feels much more predictable with stronger immigration enforcement.

In times of despair we tend to look for an all-powerful leader who will magically provide food and drink and peaceful pasture. The many thousands of people stuck in airports when a volcanic eruption or massive thunderstorm stymies air travel yearn for that sort of help.

At other times, even in the face of significant challenges, we may look for a friend and companion who will walk alongside and share the work of leading—like two climbers who alternate the technical work of leading sections of a climb up an overhanging rock face—or the shared leadership of healthy long-term marriages.

What sort of leader we're willing to follow—or befriend—has something to do with our current situation in life. Jesus as a good shepherd feeds, waters, and protects his sheep. But the phrase "good shepherd" would have been a contradiction in terms in Jesus' day. The reality is that shepherds were scorned losers—unclean, both literally and figuratively, and unwelcome in any kind of upstanding citizen's home or neighborhood.

Think about the cattle ranchers of the old American West, who thought sheepherders were lower than rustlers. They claimed that sheep destroyed the grazing land, and sheepherders frequently turned up dead. A hundred years ago, many Basque immigrants went from the borderlands of France and Spain to the high deserts of the West to herd sheep. Today they come from Peru and other points south. You can see their carvings in the aspen trees of northern Nevada, illustrating the boredom and loneliness they endured for months and years on end.

There's a forty-mile trail in one mountain range, where every time the sheep stopped to graze a shepherd had an opportunity to sharpen his knife and mark his passing—dozens of times, mile after mile. You can still see his etchings today: "*Antonio Hidalgo, peruano, borreguero, con muchos cojones y poco dinero.*" Antonio Hidalgo, Peruvian, shepherd, with plenty of guts but no cash.

Shepherds in Jesus' day were essentially homeless. They didn't have any permanent place to lay their head at night. They spent their days and nights in the open, rarely bathed, carried sick sheep to safety, and probably dispatched the sickest. One pastor recently shared his opinion that in the first century, a shepherd's more likely response to Jesus' story of ninety-nine sheep who stuck around and one who strayed would have been to break the neck of the wanderer—too much trouble to pastor that one!

Each morning shepherds had to sort out their sheep and goats from the others who shared the open grazing land, and they had to take on various predators, both animal and human. The competing shepherds in common grazing lands had to be able to tell their sheep apart—each shepherd knew the sheep as individuals and had a distinctive call to gather his own; the sheep of that herd knew that call, and followed their own shepherd.

Many of the ancients thought of shepherds as thieves, probably because of confusion among the sheep on those common pastures. There's even a prohibition in Jewish law against buying wool and milk from shepherds, lest one unwittingly receive stolen goods. Shepherds weren't considered reliable as witnesses, and couldn't give testimony.

Why would anyone want to follow somebody like that? Why would Jesus call himself a shepherd?

Maybe this is why: This good shepherd Jesus hangs out with anybody and everybody, and joins the outcasts and the forgotten. This isn't sanitary Jesus, robed in Mr. Clean whites and looking saintly on an old stained-glass window. This is Hell's Angel Jesus on a Harley, rounding up toys for poor kids. This is gang leader Jesus, pushing his homeys to fill an old lady's grocery cart, and then haul it home for her and put the food away. This is a shepherd like Oscar Romero—the bishop of El Salvador who spoke out against injustice and was assassinated in 1980—challenging the government to remember those who are left out.

This kind of shepherd comes in surprising guises, speaking in unfamiliar tongues, but leading us toward a society marked by welcome for all, where there's room at the table for people of every family, language, and nation—because it's God's table, not ours.

Jesus the good shepherd wipes away tears from every eye, finds shelter for all out of the scorching sun, waters them in the desert at the springs of the water of life, and feeds every single one on the borderless pasture planted and grown for all of God's beloved creatures, not just a privileged few. That's a shepherd worth following.

For Reflection

Think about the unexpected places and guises in which you've seen the good shepherd at work in your life and your community.

Part Four

Connecting with the Heart of God

What does it really mean to say that God lived among us in human flesh? The challenge for followers of Jesus is to connect with him on a human level as a brother, a teacher, a holy example, a shepherd, and also to connect with God on a more than human level. We're invited, encouraged, even *lured* into relationship with love, and then to live as that sort of love in the world.

Who Is Jesus in the World Today?

And the Word became flesh and lived among us, and we have seen his glory, the glory as of a father's only son, full of grace and truth.

—JOHN 1:14

For Christians, our faith begins with the reality of incarnation—not as a son of Caesar, in political and military power, but as a babe born to a poor and homeless couple on the run. God chooses to make the divine reality known in a poor child, born to an oppressed people, in a marginal land. The God who comes from underneath to change the world already gives evidence of the nature of the divine in those simple realities. The reality of incarnation begins in humility and smallness and ends by changing the order of the cosmos.

So our faith begins with Jesus of Nazareth rather than with the Messiah—the Christ—of generations and millennia to come. We begin with the child who grows up learning a trade from his father, learning to be a *tekton*, as he would have been called in Greek—the best translation for that is probably something like handyman, architect, or practical engineer.

Jesus of Nazareth shares our human condition—its deprivation and scandal, its joy and suffering. He knows all the insult, shame, and messiness of the human condition, and ultimately chooses life at every turn—the kind of life, in a larger understanding, that leads to more of itself: the *abundant life* for which he says he came among us. Healing, feeding, taking counsel with the ordinary people around him, Jesus subverts the ways of the world that assume that power lies in control and subjugation.

The friend we have in Jesus offers strength, courage, and example when we are confronted by the arrogant urge to be first—the push to be first in line, first through the traffic light or onto the off-ramp, first in the number of toys we possess or the size of our bank accounts. Jesus points in the other direction, telling us to look to the last in line and discover the sacred right there in patience, endurance, and the ability to ignore the emptiness of power mongering. He points us to the possibilities of those who are last in line, gathering to make feast in nearly empty homes, rejoicing at the presence of visitors, and feeding them even if they must stint themselves.

The man from Galilee with whom Christians try to walk shows us something essential about being a child of God—and an adult of God—deeply involved in the dailiness of human life. He worked with his hands. He engaged anyone who wanted to engage or encounter him, including the religious leaders of his time, the Pharisees; the local Roman leader, Pilate; the sick and outcast—lepers (including the ones who didn't thank him for his healing touch), the blind, women of scandalous reputation, and petty and crooked local functionaries. He didn't discriminate or avoid people on the basis of their position or their occupation, their gender or their family relationship. The only privilege he offered was for those in need, healing the woman who had been hemorrhaging for seven long years (Mark 5:25–29) and the paralytic whose friends lowered him down to Jesus by cutting a hole through the roof (Mark 2:1–12).

And at the same time, Jesus never hesitated to go apart for some time alone—to go up the mountain to pray or to sit in a boat to find a little distance. His ministry of presence also required absence. That absence has something to do with the ability to disconnect from the world's adulation or critique and rediscover our beloved-ness in God.

The stories of Jesus' baptism are singularly important to the way Christians understand and relate to him. Jesus' baptism by John, in the waters of the Jordan, was transformative. He enters that living water of rebirth, and as he emerges, he hears the divine voice pro-claiming his belovedness. Jesus, the living Word, hears the word of God, and in some Christian understandings, he becomes the Word at that moment, in that hearing, recognizing his vocation or partic-ipation in that Word.

"You are my beloved, and in you I am well pleased." If we're will-ing to risk hearing that and being transformed by it, we have begun to participate in Jesus' reality. It is a hopeful saying for most of us—we don't quite believe that we can be all that pleasing to God, because we think we know more about ourselves than God does. But it was also an aspiration in Jesus' ears—he aspired to live into the fullness of God's intent.

In Mark 10:37, Jesus challenges his disciples about participating in his baptism when James and John start asking for preferment: "Who's going to get to sit next to you in your kingdom?" If they had chosen belovedness over competition, they wouldn't have needed to ask the question. The ability to see ourselves as beloved, above and before all else, is foundational. It is what Paul of Tarsus is getting at in his letter to the Romans when he asks, "Who will separate us from the love of Christ, who died and was raised, who is at the right hand of God and intercedes for us? Nothing," he answers, "will be able to separate us from the love of God in Christ Jesus our Lord." When we live deeply immersed in that reality, when we have been steeped in the transformative bath, we are more able to choose a different course—by knowing the reality of God's grace.

Right after his baptism, Jesus heads out to the wilderness. Knowing himself beloved is at the root of Jesus' retreats—going up the mountain, going fishing (or at least messing about in boats), and spending nights on beaches and in gardens. Those retreats are about intentionally reconnecting with the source of all that is, of all life and love, abundance, goodness, beauty, and grace. That deep knowledge of our own belovedness only comes of awareness, and awareness is cultivated by attention—attending to the divine in careful, intentional ways. Jesus doesn't seek permission for going apart. And he doesn't just give us permission to do the same. He insists on it. His retreats, whether they're quiet or active wrestling matches, are at the root of his ability to know his mission: "Love God with all you are, and love your neighbor as yourself." We can't love God without spending time and attending to the evidence of God around us and within us, and we can't love anybody else without that.

What did Jesus encounter up the mountain, and out in the boat, and in the long night in the garden? I keep going to those places, and to other places apart, looking to be reminded. I find utter awe at the beauty of creation, of the love of God for each and every part of it, in the old eternal rocks, the birds of the air, the tiny plants putting out brave flowers in barren gravel far above the treeline, and in the unimagined beauty of little squid that never see the light of day, but instead put out their own flashes of light from organs like jewels in the starlight. I see the belovedness of all creation.

If we're willing, Jesus will lead us into other solitary places such as the garden on the Mount of Olives, to confront our own avoidance of pain, let go of the sense of betrayal, or find an easier way through the hard work of love. We can ask our friends to go along with us, but the best they can do is watch our backs. They can't do the work of "being" for us. That's something each of us must do, on our own, in our own wilderness.

The *tekton* or construction worker from Nazareth built things— fences, stone walls, maybe even coffins. But he also built community. We don't know much about his craft, but we do know that it was useful—it contributed in some way to the life of the community around him. He called others to join him who did similarly constructive things. There were Andrew and the fishing sons of Zebedee; Mary and Martha of Bethany, cooks and providers of gracious hospitality; Zacchaeus the tree surgeon; Peter's mother-in-law, who rises from her sickbed to care for her guests. One was even a tax collector and Roman collaborator—and all found themselves part of Jesus' "family." Jesus dignified all manner of work, including Mary of Bethany's desire to just sit still, while her sister was rushing around, and learn through conversation.

Jesus was a teacher—a rabbi—as well as a healer and a feeder. The rabbi looked after his community by challenging their understandings and encouraging their continued growth. Jesus as rabbi is connected to the way some of the gospels characterize him, as child of Wisdom and Wisdom's prophet (Luke 2:40). There is an aspect of following Jesus that is about sharing what we have learned from our encounters with grace. It's connected to the great commission to go and tell the good news we know, but it's also a divine urge beyond any settled knowing. God's invitation, the road we know in Jesus, leads us onward. Like him, we're not meant to have a place to lay our head until, at the last, we find our rest in God. There's an innate restlessness that keeps us searching for "the hand of God at work in the world about us,"[1] and a similar invitation to meet Jesus on the road. Seeing Jesus as the "hand of God at work in the world" echoes the ancient understanding of Wisdom as God's master-builder, present from creation, helping to craft creation. Jesus is himself a master-builder, a *tekton* before he became an itinerant healer and teacher. He is indeed creation's architect incarnate, making the design of creation evident in human flesh.

God's intent for creation is made evident in words, as well. The part of Jesus' rabbinic ministry that challenges the unlovely ways in which creation has been or is being misused is shared with the ancient tradition of the Hebrew prophets, who speak in God's name to confront the evil of the world around us, and—equally in God's name—to the vision of God for a restored and reconciled world.

Jesus' first act of ministry in Luke's gospel is to read from Isaiah in his home synagogue. He claims the ancient prophetic vision of *shalom*, of creation restored, when captives are set free, the blind are healed, and the oppressed receive justice. He claims his own work as restoring to community, healing the breach, and bringing the captives home when he says to the assembled congregation, "Today this scripture has been fulfilled in your hearing" (Luke 4:21). And he goes on to live out that promise, feeding the hungry, healing the sick and dispossessed, and repeatedly bringing the marginalized into the center of the community. The prisoners he frees are the people who have been walled out of community, including the mentally ill fellow who's living in the tombs (Mark 5:3), or the leper who must walk around crying out, "unclean, unclean—don't come near me, I'm unclean" in Leviticus 13:45 and Matthew 8:2. In healing them he begins to free the prisoners inside a particular community as well, by opening the gates and expanding the table, quite literally feeding thousands. The challenging encounters at the end of his ministry are about healing the larger structures of injustice—overturning the tables in the temple and challenging the powers of his world, especially the power of the Roman Empire, with greater claims to truth and justice.

Jesus' work as prophet, particularly as a prophet of God's imminent and ultimate reign, is central to his identity, and central to his call to his followers. This is the vision that drives my ministry, and where I think I'm called to follow. Jesus' ministry of teaching, healing, and table fellowship is about God's heavenly banquet, and the discipled life is about answering the summons of Jesus to transform the brokenness of this world. That is the Christian vocation.

The Greek word behind "call," the root of the Latin *vocare*, from which our word *vocation* comes, shares a common root with the word for beauty, virtue, and goodness, so that understanding one's call is about answering what is good and noble. The word for church comes from the same root—the church is the people of God, who are called toward that vision of ultimate beauty and virtue, that divine vision of a restored and reconciled creation. When Jesus says, "I am the way, and the truth, and the life" (John 14:6), he is talking about vocation. In answering the summons to walk the Jesus road— responding to our vocation—we discover what is truly beautiful, the life abundant for which God destined all of creation, the truly good life that is possible when all creation is in right relationship.

The life abundant for which all were created, before time and forever, is bound up in living together in abundance and peace, in right relationship with God and all others. It is God's mission, in which the Church participates. It is the grace with which the cosmos was created. Jesus' urgency is to share that vision and reality with those around him. He died for that—for announcing that coming kingdom, for showing signs of its immanent presence, and for imaging and imagining its possibility. He was killed for that vision, and his life, ministry, death, and resurrection made it evident. The followers of Jesus are both heirs of that kingdom and its builders. We are meant to build what the divine architect has set before us.

Do we know ourselves beloved? Then we must go and act like it, helping others discover their own belovedness, so that they too are caught up in the heart of God. Our work is to build a society of justice where all can live as God's beloved—as friends of God incarnate.

Consider the image of Jesus as shepherd. I have on my desk, where I work in New York, an old postcard that shows a Navajo shepherd. It's from a black and white photograph taken in 1925 near Shiprock, New Mexico. Most of the sky is covered with dark clouds, but there is light on the horizon. The herd isn't all that big, but it has white sheep and black sheep, sheep with long hair and short, lambs and old ones. The shepherd is looking out over the backs of her sheep far into the distance. That picture—that image—offers both reassurance and invitation to me, reminder that the good shepherd has all of us in his ken, and yet each one of those sheep, each of us, is called to similar kinds of shepherding on his behalf.

I want to follow the Jesus who descended into hell, the one who turned hell upside down looking for Judas. I want to follow the Jesus who went to the graveyard and invited Lazarus back into life. I want to follow the Jesus who went to the temple and turned over the market stalls. I want to follow the Jesus who gave hope to the crook who hung on the next cross. I want to follow the Jesus who was willing to be taught by a foreign woman that he was supposed to give *her* good news, too. And I want to follow the Jesus who hung out with the wrong people, and challenged the "right people" to reexamine their definitions and priorities.

None of us can do that alone; we need the friend and fellow sheepherder we find—and connect with—in Jesus, who connects us with the heart of God.

For Reflection

What image of Jesus keeps you company on the road? What image keeps you yearning and growing and following?

Finding Our Way Home

I have other sheep that do not belong to this fold. I must bring them also, and they will listen to my voice. So there will be one flock, one shepherd.

—JOHN 10:16

In The Episcopal Church, we work with many partners around the world, and with other denominations and faith traditions. One of the great gifts of ecumenical work is discovering new facets on the old jewels of our faith. From the Moravian Church, I've learned to be grateful for and intrigued by the festival celebration of Jesus as Chief Elder, which recognizes Jesus as the chief shepherd of the entire church—the body of Christ. Taking part in this festival reminds me that the first line of my job description says "chief pastor" to The Episcopal Church—a completely impossible task, and an aspiration that tends toward hubris.

A significant portion of the responsibility of any pastor has to do with protecting the flock. As Jesus notes, the shepherd must guard against those who try to get in by ways other than the gate (John 10:1–2). Any human shepherd needs others to help with that work, because the shepherd is just one person, with limited capacity and limited vision. A growing number of shepherds and goatherds in the United States use llamas as flock guardians. That exotic creature is so big that dogs and coyotes and rustlers all take a second look before they try to sneak in to harass the sheep.

127

Sometimes the local protector is even a member of the flock. My husband and I kept goats in Oregon for more than twenty years, and I still have vivid memories of an early summer morning when a wandering dog got into the pasture. The dog was kept at bay by a big wether, a castrated male goat, who outweighed the other goats by a good fifty pounds. He protected the rest of the herd until the human goatherd got there, but he was mortally wounded in the process. That happens to human shepherds as well.

Christians look to the model of the good shepherd, who lays his life down for others, who exists to serve, who knows all by name, and who loves each member of the flock equally. We all have the ability to look out for one another—it's part of the pastoral task that all God's people share, for each of us is shepherd as well as sheep. Episcopalians talk a lot about baptismal ministry, which includes the need to respect the dignity of every human being, and working for justice, freedom, and peace. When every single person is met with justice and dignity, it's a lot harder for predators to get into the pasture. When the sheep are working at finding the mind of Jesus, the herd might even begin to turn the predators into vegetarians.

The Franciscans have a wonderful understanding of the finite nature of pastoral ministry. They describe it in four acts: show up, pay attention, tell the truth, and leave the results to God. Be present and alert in your pastoral ministry, be faithful in sharing the results of your discernment, and let God be God.

Yet keeping the sheep safe doesn't mean restraining them forever in one pasture. Sheep need exercise and varied grazing to stay healthy. A good shepherd keeps the sheep moving, from one foraging spot to another. A herd that remains too long in one pasture becomes far more liable to infection with parasites and disease. It is the risk of journeying beyond the familiar and known that contributes to health—and a varied diet provides far better nutrition. The dangers do not only come from outside. Abundant life requires venturing beyond the corral.

Life outside the familiar pasture can be challenging—and the many conversations among Christian faith communities about full communion with one another are wonderful examples. We are only beginning to discover the abundance of other pastures, and we have little sense of the blessings they will bring to each of our varied communities. The good shepherd himself acknowledged the reality of many flocks, but only one shepherd. He pointed out that there were herds his hearers didn't know about, but he was meant to tend them as well. Our own ecumenical adventures are small steps toward that reality.

Not too long ago, I visited Grace Montessori School in Allentown, Pennsylvania. Though it's located in a parking garage—an unlikely pasture for lambs!—this learning community brings together children from a broad variety of cultural backgrounds. These young children had made a booklet for me, with a picture of their class and their names, one page for each class. On the cover was a picture of Jesus with a lamb. I asked the children who he was, and why he had a sheep, and they responded, "He's found the lost one." As we looked through the pictures, the children pointed out their names, written in the beginning printing of three- to six-year-olds. There was some pathos as one little girl couldn't find her own name. But no one is lost—we found it on the edge of a page, tucked into the fold. All those kids know they have a place, and that each of them is known by name. The teacher's hauntingly beautiful recounting of the story of the good shepherd reminded them once again: This shepherd will find you when you're feeling lost; this shepherd will call your name and lead you home.

We share that task, all of us, whatever pasture we call home. Our chief and elder brother—our good shepherd—names each one of us, always leading us toward a broader meadow, always leading us home to God.

For Reflection

When have you been lost? Who helped lead you home?

Stardust

Remember that you are dust, and to dust you shall return.
—BOOK OF COMMON PRAYER, PAGE 265

One of my favorite cartoons is of a priest imposing ashes and saying, "Remember that you are dust, but a very fine kind of dust." It is true, for we are God's creatures, created from the earth, made of the same dust that comes ultimately from the stars. At the same time we are sinners, too, and we are made in the image of God. It may be good spiritual practice to recall our sinful past, but God will never let us forget that we are created in God's image.

We are dust, given life by the spirit of God. We are dust, hoping to be worthy of the image of God. Regular spiritual practice gives us a chance to recall our vocation, a vocation that we find on the road toward God. As sacks of dust, on our pilgrimage to the reign of God, we need to start our training, as athletes do. But this training is for life, not just for a game.

Our training is with the other members of the Christian team, including the rookies who are just beginning to learn about Jesus. Both old and new Christians need to recover the practices of our faith—self-examination and repentance, prayer, fasting, self-denial, and reading and meditating on scripture.

Self-examination is essentially a call to nurture an open heart that can hear the voice or the spirit of God. In the very first sentence of the Rule of Benedict, the monastic guidebook written in the sixth century and still in use today, monks are instructed to listen carefully to God and "incline the ear of your heart" toward the divine. We too need to ask ourselves about how we are listening to God with the ear of *our* heart. Prayer, more than anything else, is the ability, the aim, and the desire to hear the spirit of God. Having heard the spirit, whenever we perceive something wrong or closed within ourselves, and then return to the path once again, we are doing repentance. The word *penitence* means to return to God. No more, no less.

Fasting and self-denial are spiritual exercises designed not just to help us lose a few pounds and achieve better physical health. They are also signs of our participation in the body of God's creation. Our hungers and desires, whatever they may be, affect our sisters and brothers. Whenever we consume too much food, water, energy, carbon, or space, we impact them negatively. We are telling others that they are not worth as much as we are. We are denying that they, too, reflect the image of God. For this reason, the spiritual practice of fasting offers us an opportunity to value our neighbors as ourselves, and it is a good way to increase our capacity for loving them.

Reading and meditating on the word of God is another opportunity to hear the spirit. We need to focus on the history of our faith, especially the story of God's love for all creation, and the life, passion, and resurrection of Jesus.

This spiritual work is our opportunity to bless the dust from which we're made so that it can shine even brighter than the stars—like the light of Jesus. Our world needs that light, resurrected from dust.

Remember that we are dust, and to dust we shall return—dust of the earth and of heaven.

For Reflection

How can we increase our capacity to hear, and to turn back toward the kingdom of God? How can we live with love for all people?

The Dream of God

Truly I tell you, just as you did it to one of the least of these who are members of my family, you did it to me.

—MATTHEW 25:40

Christians are part of a really big extended family. And each time we gather to worship, we gave thanks for the many saints who have come before us, for our ancestors and our brothers and sisters in the faith, for all who have toiled to build the world we have dreamed of, the dream the prophets—both ancient and modern—continue to hold before us, the world we have not yet seen in its fullness.

Moses led his people out of slavery in Egypt in search of that dream, toward a land of milk and honey, where bondage would be left behind, where no one's labor would be stolen by the powerful, where God's children might live in peace and abundance. It's the same dream that the prophet Martin Luther King Jr. held before us—a world where no one goes hungry, each person has a decent shelter at night, and all have an equal claim on justice. It is the eternal dream of God's spirit within us, and it is the vision Jesus urges on his followers. This dream isn't just a dream for the end time. It comes among us like a thief in the night, it sneaks up on us when we're not paying attention, and it lives within us.

We confronted that dream as we saw the terror of the earthquake in Haiti, a land shaken by the impersonal forces of an ever-changing globe. But human forces, too, play an enormous role in the terror in that island nation. In the midst of all the devastation, though—both natural and human-made—the dream of God has been evident in the care of one Haitian for another, and in the care of the world's urgent response.

Most of the buildings of the Episcopal Diocese of Haiti in and around Port-au-Prince were destroyed, and four people were killed at worship in a church in an outlying area. Bishop Zaché Duracin organized a camp of several thousand persons on a soccer field, tending to those with nowhere to go. They were given water and some food, and a purpose—to care for one another and for the suffering around them. The dream of God became real on that soccer field, in small and not-so-hidden ways.

Still, watching the news reports in January 2010, our hearts broke as we saw the bodies and heard the stories about the mothers, fathers, and children who didn't know where their family members were. The recovery and rebuilding will take a very long time. The damage in Haiti is far worse than it was when an equivalent earthquake hit San Francisco twenty years ago, when only sixty-two people died, because the infrastructure in Haiti is so poor and the buildings there so fragile. The extreme devastation is largely a result of Haiti's extreme poverty.

That poverty is what the prophet Martin Luther King would challenge us about. Haiti has its roots in a history of slavery—Spaniards first imported Africans as slaves there in 1517. The island went back and forth between Spanish and French control during the next two centuries, with the French eventually colonizing the western part. In 1804, a slave revolt led to the first independent nation in Latin America, the second independent nation in this hemisphere, the first post-colonial black-led nation anywhere in the world, and the first nation established as the result of a successful slave rebellion. If that isn't an Exodus story, I don't know what is. The Haitians were delivered from Pharoah, led by their own team of Moseses. Yet they have never tasted much milk and honey.

The prophets would remind us that there are still slaves around us—those who live in thralldom to grinding poverty, including the 80 percent of Haitians who live on less than two dollars a day. That's the kind of poverty that the first of the Millennium Development Goals is meant to relieve. The prophets would remind us that there is no justice when some people live in this kind of poverty. And the prophet Martin Luther King Jr. would remind us, as the Hebrew prophets once did, that the people of Haiti are our brothers and sisters. Consider his words:

> How can one avoid being depressed when he sees with his own eyes evidences of millions of people going to bed hungry at night? How can one avoid being depressed when he sees with his own eyes God's children sleeping on the sidewalks at night? Injustice anywhere is a threat to justice everywhere. We are tied together in a single garment of destiny, caught in an inescapable network of mutuality.
> —LETTER FROM BIRMINGHAM JAIL, APRIL 16, 1963

Martin Luther King's ministry was focused on liberating the people of the United States, but his message pointed toward the universal liberation of all people, all God's children, here in our country and all around the globe. The work he began here helped liberate the people of South Africa. The ways Americans and faithful people around the world began to hear that universal message have made us conscious that oppression, discrimination, and injustice anywhere are indeed *our* problem. We are most certainly "caught in an inescapable network of mutuality."

When Christians—indeed all people of faith—are abundantly aware of that reality, they show it in care for and ministry with those who suffer in want of food, clothing, shelter, and education. A particular focus on children remembers that Jesus, after all, came among us as one of them, and just might remind us that we're all God's children and Jesus is still present among us in the most vulnerable.

What do we do when we encounter someone who is particularly vulnerable? We've all seen and heard the stories about rescue workers trying to get still-living people out of ruined buildings in Haiti. One man was sedated before they dragged him through a very tight spot. Others have had water piped to them through tiny hoses. Some have had to have limbs amputated in order to deliver them from potential tombs. Rescuers do what's most needed to sustain life.

I'm struck by the image of a tiny child, newly delivered, perhaps the most vulnerable life most of us ever meet. What do we do? Wrap the child up and keep her warm. Martin Luther King invited us as the church to become a thermostat, rather than a thermometer—to be an instrument that changes the temperature of the society around us. I think it's time to turn the heat up. Babies are dying out there. God's children, our brothers and sisters, are dying of neglect—our neglect to work for justice both here and around the globe. Haiti is also a child of God, teetering on the cusp of life. She needs water, food, solidarity in prayer, work for justice, redevelopment. She needs milk and honey.

Haiti is a bellwether for the world's children, and for all God's children, caught in that network of mutuality. None of us will arrive in that land of milk and honey, of which we have dreamed for eons, none of us will enter that land until and unless we cross the river together—only hand in hand with our neighbors—the poor, the hungry, the thirsty—only when we keep on building that network of mutuality. Only then can we make God's dream a reality.

For Reflection

How do you see God's dream at work in your community?

Called by Name

[Jesus and his disciples] came to Jericho. As he and his disciples and a large crowd were leaving Jericho, Bartimaeus son of Timaeus, a blind beggar, was sitting by the roadside. When he heard that it was Jesus of Nazareth, he began to shout out and say, "Jesus, Son of David, have mercy on me!" Many sternly ordered him to be quiet, but he cried out even more loudly, "Son of David, have mercy on me!" Jesus stood still and said, "Call him here." And they called the blind man, saying to him, "Take heart; get up, he is calling you." So throwing off his cloak, he sprang up and came to Jesus. Then Jesus said to him, "What do you want me to do for you?" The blind man said to him, "My teacher, let me see again." Jesus said to him, "Go; your faith has made you well." Immediately he regained his sight and followed him on the way.

—MARK 10:46–52

Did somebody call you by name when you turned up at the breakfast table or arrived at work this morning? If so, it probably reminded you that you are a valued member of a family and a community. If not, it probably felt like something was missing. Most of us go looking for places where we can be recognized as unique human beings, and valued by the larger community. That's what good marriages are about, and long-term partnerships, and even social clubs. Being known and named is crucial to being a whole human being.

When we celebrate the sacrament of baptism, one of the first things that happens is to name those about to be baptized. We ask the sponsors to present a child by name and we call adults by name when we ask, "Do you desire to be baptized?" Naming is absolutely central to being brought into Jesus' fellowship.

In the Bible, naming is a very big deal. In the Hebrew Scriptures, Job—after a series of unfortunate incidents that sorely try his faith—is restored to health at last, and long after the death of his children, his wife bears ten more, seven sons and three daughters (Job 42:13–14). The absolutely revolutionary thing is that the daughters are named while the sons are not, and the daughters receive a share of their father's inheritance along with their brothers. It is almost as though Jemimah, Keziah, and Keren-happuch, just by being named, are recognized as equal to the sons. It is a striking thing in Job's culture, for in the ancient world daughters were usually treated as property. It may be a hint of how Job's own life is being healed, and how that healing is spreading out into the relationships around him.

Consider also the blind beggar in the gospel of Mark. Jesus heals lots of people in the gospels, but, male or female, they are almost never named. They may be identified by relationship—Simon Peter's mother-in-law, for example, or the daughter of Jairus, or the centurion's servant—but more often they are only identified by their illness: the woman with a hemorrhage, the ten lepers, the boy with a demon, a blind man.

But this blind man is named Bar-Timaeus, son of Timaeus, and he calls Jesus by a parallel name, Son of David (Mark 10:48). He has claimed a relationship with Jesus by what he calls him—a name like his own, but also a name that speaks of the healing of the whole nation hoped for in the reign of Jesus' ancestor, King David. This act of naming seems to be a central part of Bartimaeus' healing—he is called by name and he recognizes and names Jesus as Messiah.

When Jesus was baptized, he was named in relationship to God, as he heard a voice from the heavens proclaim, "You are my Son, the

Beloved; with you I am well pleased" (Mark 1:11). His identity is *beloved*—and his relationship is *pleasing to God*. The heavenly voice doesn't say, "I will be well pleased with you when you're done with your work." Instead, it insists that right at this moment God is *already* well pleased.

Bartimaeus begins his journey to healing by calling out to Jesus, demanding his attention, and claiming a relationship. He's a lot like an aggressive panhandler—"I need two bucks for a hamburger, right now!" The people around him try to shut him up, but he's too insistent and obnoxious for Jesus to ignore. Jesus hears him and calls him over, acknowledging the relationship, and asking Bartimaeus what he wants. "Let me see again," Bartimaeus responds. With that he is healed and begins to follow Jesus *on the way*. That's gospel-speak for joining Jesus on the road that leads home to God.

This is almost the only time in the gospels when a healed person joins Jesus as a disciple. Usually, the people Jesus heals just go on their merry way—except the leper who comes back for a minute to say thank you. The only other person who sticks around after being healed is Mary of Magdala—and, like the other disciples around Jesus, we know her name. She becomes the first witness to the resurrection, the apostle who goes to tell the others the news that Jesus lives. We're told Bartimaeus' name because he's a disciple—a follower of Jesus *on the way*.

This is the very last person Jesus heals in Mark's gospel. Jesus is about to enter Jerusalem and walk through his last few days. The way or the road that Bartimaeus joins is the same road that leads to Calvary and the cross—and eventually, also, to resurrection. It's a road that can't tolerate anonymous strangers.

Becoming a disciple has an essential connection with being named. Being known by name—John or Jane, Mitsuko or Michael—means being recognized as a beloved child of God and as a friend. Being called by name is essential to getting on the road. We don't travel with strangers. We need every friend we can find.

My husband climbed Denali twenty years ago. He spent months working together with three other guys, planning and getting equipment ready, training themselves, and building a team. They knew each other pretty well by the time they set off for Alaska. They spent almost a month on that mountain, and the friendship began to fray. They didn't know each other as well as they thought they did, and when individual fears and foibles began to surface, the team began to disintegrate. They all got off the mountain safely, but not together, and they didn't all even try to go to the top. For all four of them, their safety and their lives depended on the friends they kept and the new ones they made on that mountain.

Jesus' road is tougher than Denali. It's more treacherous, and more joyous. We need to know our companions.

Hiking Jesus' road means we really have to want to see—to see the world in all its wretchedness and in all its glory. Like Bartimaeus, we have to be willing to shout out for those who need healing—and sometimes it will be us. We have to let go of the old comfortable security blankets that we've depended on in our blindness.

We have to know our own names, and the names of our companions on the journey. All those names start with *beloved*, and *pleasing to God*, and *friend*. Called by name, we respond deeply to our relationship with God.

For Reflection

When were you surprised to be called by name? What effect did it have?

The Web of Life

As they were going along the road, they came to some water; and the eunuch said, "Look, here is water! What is to prevent me from being baptized?" He commanded the chariot to stop, and both of them, Philip and the eunuch, went down into the water, and Philip baptized him. When they came up out of the water, the Spirit of the Lord snatched Philip away; the eunuch saw him no more, and went on his way rejoicing. But Philip found himself at Azotus, and as he was passing through the region, he proclaimed the good news to all the towns until he came to Caesarea.

—ACTS 8:36–40

I recently attended a meeting of the Anglican Communion in Jamaica, and while I was there, the news each day told of violent deaths: a fire-bombing where an eighty-five-year-old woman was burned to death; a middle-aged businesswoman shot to death as she came home from work and tried to remove her grandson from the car; the body of a ten-year-old girl found in the brush behind her home a few days after she disappeared. They are very much like the deaths reported each day in cities and nations across the globe. All those deaths leave big holes in the web of life. Those lives have been stolen from the treasure of families and human communities.

Sometimes connections to that web of life are severed in other ways. There was news recently of two women, born in a hospital in Oregon on the same day in 1956. DNA tests have just proven that they were sent home with the wrong mothers. They're beginning to realize that their lives and identities are based on error.

In the very early days of the church, the apostle Philip, traveling on the road to Gaza, meets an Ethiopian man who may seem hale and hearty, but as a eunuch he, too, has been cut off from the web of life. In the ancient world, people counted their significance in offspring, descendants who would carry on their name and story for generations to come. The eunuch has quite literally been cut off from those generations, and from a place in the community that might have given him value and meaning. He is clearly an important official—he has been trusted with the queen's treasury and he's able to take expensive transport to Jerusalem and buy a costly scroll. But his connection to that web of life was stolen from him as a child or a young man, in much the same way that the culture and livelihood of Native Americans were stolen away from them. They were systematically cut off from the web of life and from the land that gave meaning, so that their lands might be used for somebody else's purposes. In the ancient world, eunuchs were made so for somebody else's purposes, too—to look after the royal harem (the word *eunuch* literally means something like "guardian of the bed").

In the ancient world, eunuchs were also cut off from the religious community. In the Hebrew Scriptures, the book of Deuteronomy (23:1) excludes them from the worshiping assembly, though by the time of the prophet Isaiah, hundreds of years later, eunuchs are welcome: "To the eunuchs who keep my sabbaths ... I will give [them] an everlasting name that shall not be cut off" (Isaiah 56:4–5).

Still, a eunuch had few ties or links to the web of meaning and humanity and loving-kindness. He was largely alone, and though he might be a valued and trusted officer, his social definition remained strictly in his physical condition. This story in Acts of the Apostles that details Philip's meeting with the Ethiopian eunuch doesn't even give him a name. And without a name or relatives or descendants in the ancient world, you were pretty invisible; when you died, you simply disappeared. There would be no one to remember you or tell your story.

But the court official Philip meets is looking for other connections. He has heard of the God of Abraham and Isaac, and even though he's an outsider, he's gone to worship in Jerusalem, where he might have been permitted in the outer courts of the Temple. He's bought a scroll and he's reading those life-giving assurances of the prophet Isaiah, and he's sensed the connection between his own condition and the suffering servant Isaiah writes about: "Like a lamb that is led to the slaughter, and like a sheep that before its shearers is silent, so he did not open his mouth. By a perversion of justice he was taken away. Who could have imagined his future? For he was cut off from the land of the living, stricken for the transgression of my people" (Isaiah 53:7–8). In the sight of the world, the eunuch's life has also been taken away.

He asks Philip, "Is Isaiah talking about himself or about somebody else—like, maybe, me?" So Philip begins to tell the story of another man without a traditional family. He recounts the good news about Jesus, whose family is not defined by DNA or offspring, but consists of those who love God and one another. Maybe Philip told the eunuch that it's possible to be reconnected to the web of life, immersed once again in the living stream. Maybe he told the eunuch that Jesus is the way that happens. Perhaps Philip said that from now on, the eunuch doesn't have to be alone, isolated, without meaning or relationship—that he can be part of a body that does not die, that will live forever.

Whatever Philip says, the royal treasurer seems to get it. "Here's some water," he points out. "Baptize me now! I want to be part of that ever-flowing stream of relationships. I want to be part of a family that lives beyond this life, of connections that last for eternity."

When they come up out of the water, the royal treasurer goes on his way rejoicing. He has discovered the treasure now planted within him, a treasure to watch over and guard, not to keep safely hidden away. He goes home and shares that treasure with his fellow Ethiopians, where Christians in that African land still count this baptism as the beginning of their church. When the first missionaries went to Sudan a couple of hundred years ago, they found evidence of the treasurer's work seventeen or eighteen centuries earlier. The Sudanese also count him as their first apostle. Truly, his name has lived on, and indeed he has many descendants in that place to this day.

Whose story do *we* tell? Whose child are we, whose sister or brother? How is our identity carried on? Our job is to give thanks for the gift of all our relatives—our sisters and brothers and mothers and fathers in Jesus, in whom we discover life that endures even beyond the grave. We can give thanks for the lives of those who've been snatched away from the web of life in this place, and keep telling their stories. But that's only the beginning.

Our common task is to challenge this family of God to reach out and connect those who are cut off, who believe themselves abandoned. That royal treasurer didn't respond to his amputation with violence, but too many of our brothers and sisters do. The violence around us is a result of not seeing the treasure in our midst—the treasure of a family that can reach beyond bonds of blood to those of love.

The people around the royal treasurer, and many of the Jews with whom he would have rubbed elbows in Jerusalem, likely saw him as a problem, a man without a family or a "normal" place in the world. The kinder ones may have felt sorry for him. Some may have envied his position, though not his physical state. His ultimate treasure was discovering the good news that God loved him, and that his relationship with Jesus gave him a new family, and ultimate meaning to his life. In Jesus, producing offspring to carry on your name is not the goal or meaning of life. Loving your neighbors, and recognizing them as your relations, is.

The royal treasurer has found a different treasure—not the pile of gold he's been put in charge of for the Queen of Ethiopia. He's found the treasure of God's love, a love without price or end. And it's a treasure that doesn't have to be kept locked up or kept safe—it's a treasure that grows as it's shared. It's a treasure that connects him with the heart of the web of life.

For Reflection

Who will we share treasure with? How will we reach out and touch those who are cut off from that treasure? Whom do you know who feels isolated and alone? Who is abandoned, depressed, or lost? Who needs the treasure you have? Start there. Start there, and don't stop.

Saints and Superheroes

But the souls of the righteous are in the hand of God,
and no torment will ever touch them.
In the eyes of the foolish they seemed to have died,
and their departure was thought to be a disaster,
and their going from us to be their destruction;
but they are at peace.
For though in the sight of men they were punished,
their hope is full of immortality.
Having been disciplined a little, they will receive great good,
because God tested them and found them worthy of himself;
like gold in the furnace he tried them,
and like a sacrificial burnt offering he accepted them.
In the time of their visitation they will shine forth,
and will run like sparks through the stubble.
They will govern nations and rule over peoples,
and the Lord will reign over them for ever.
Those who trust in him will understand truth,
and the faithful will abide with him in love,
because grace and mercy are upon his holy ones,
and he watches over his elect.

—WISDOM 3:1–9

Consider the saints. In the beginning, they were the great heroes
of the faith—the superheroes of the first couple of centuries of

Christianity. In the early church, on the anniversary of the death of one of those heroes, the congregation would go to the grave and celebrate Eucharist right there on the person's tomb. They did it for each of those saints, all through the year.

At some point, the community began to realize that every single one of the baptized was a saint—a holy one—each in his or her own way. And by about the fourth century there got to be too many of those superhero folk to go to the grave of each one. That's really where the feast of All Saints, which we celebrate each year on the first of November, comes from—giving thanks, and praying for, each and every Christian witness, living and dead.

The saints are people who show us what God looks like in human flesh. They're ordinary people who shows us something extraordinary—such as Mother Teresa, who tended the poorest of the poor in Calcutta; or St. Patrick, who brought the faith to Ireland and loved the people who had formerly enslaved him; or Mary, the mother of God, who answered "yes" when the challenging request came from God. Like Dietrich Bonhoeffer, who was killed for his faith by the Nazis, they are examples of selfless care for others. But when we install our saints in niches or put them up on pedestals, far away and too holy to have anything to do with common folk like us, they aren't really much good to anybody. It can feel pretty impossible to be like somebody such as that.

I'm fond of the saints who are *very* demonstrably human—such as St. Jerome. He was a fourth-century monk who translated the Bible into Latin, but he was also a famously grumpy curmudgeon, not very nice at all to be around. Maybe his famously nasty personality gave him more time to make the word of God so much more available to all Christians. And if he made it on to the list of saints, well, maybe there's hope for the rest of us.

Saints show us what holiness looks like, what it means to be whole and healed—words that come from the same root as *holy*— though not necessarily in every part of their lives. Living saints are still works in progress. They can be people who go out of their way to care for somebody else, or show us what generosity looks like. Those saints are all around us, but we may have to look hard to see them.

At one level, the saints are all baptized people, all sisters and brothers in Jesus. Consider some of the everyday saints we bump into all the time: people who foster or adopt children, for instance, wanting to see them grow up using all the gifts they've been given. There's a ninety-two-year-old woman I met recently who said her ministry was pouring lemonade—a major example of hospitality. There's the young Lakota deacon I met in Minnesota, who serves on the Episcopal Church's Executive Council, who is teaching others about how to make decisions: consider the seven generations who have come before, he advises, and the seven generations who will follow us.

That generational focus is a wonderful reminder of the reality that the saints who went before us are still very much part of us—the communion of saints we speak about every time we say the creed, the profession of faith that many Christians recite when they gather for Sunday worship. The communion of saints is the spiritual union of all Christians, both living and dead, each of them part of a single "mystical body," with Jesus as the head.

Who comes to mind as part of that communion of saints? For me, it includes the awareness I've had at the altar on occasion of a saint who has just died. The mother of a good friend, after years of illness, died on a Friday, and was palpably present when I joined another congregation for Eucharist that Sunday. She and her family had taught me something important about communion in other forms, such as crackers and soda while we sat in the emergency room.

Saints are those who make us aware of God's abundance and God's urgency. As the book of Wisdom in the Hebrew Scriptures puts it, they "run like sparks through the stubble" (3:7)—change agents in God's field. Isaiah speaks of them as participants and suppliers of the heavenly banquet, the feast spread for all God's people, a feast eaten in peace and rejoicing, when grief and mourning have passed away (Isaiah 25:6–9). Revelation reminds us that this vision of a new Jerusalem, literally, a new city of peace and rejoicing and the end of mourning, is God's dream for us all (Revelation 21:2).

The gospel story of Lazarus offers an important insight about saints. When Lazarus fell ill, his sisters, Martha and Mary, called Jesus to their village to heal him—and Jesus, arriving four days too late, weeps at the death of his friend, and then stuns the entire village by calling Lazarus out of his tomb (John 11:1–44).

Yet once Lazarus is returned to the living, the gospels don't record another word about him. He doesn't join the band of named disciples, and the gospel report of his story effectively ends. He responded to Jesus' call to come out of the tomb, and that may be all that's necessary. How many people do we know who are effectively dead—without hope or reason for living? Lazarus is a witness to how far gone you can be and still rejoin the living. The gospel is pretty graphic—he was stinking! Yet even then, corpse a-rottin'—like an alcoholic at the bottom, or a kid considering suicide—even then, more abundant life is possible. You and I just might, as saints, as witnesses to the hope that is in us, help call those Lazaruses out of the grave.

Sometimes the saints around us aren't so evidently saints. I heard a painful story about a recent encounter between Native and Anglo Episcopalians in Minnesota, as they were preparing for their bishop's consecration. A couple of Anglos were rude and dismissive to a group of Lakota people. Offended, the Native people left the preparation session—and who would blame them? Others who heard about the incident worked hard at reconciling and reminding everyone that each gift and each person was needed. Who were the Lazaruses? Probably everyone involved spent some time in that tomb, in pain and despair, not sure that any sign of life would ever be possible in the many deaths of that racist encounter. But all of them were called out of that tomb by other saints, and many have responded and are beginning to be set free.

The tombs that each of us are locked in are just as dark and filled with death and pain. Our task is to call one another out into light and life. That is the work of saints, all of us on our journey to God.

For Reflection

Where have we met Lazarus? Who will call those Lazaruses out, unbind them, and help make new life possible?

Holy Conversation

In those days Jesus came from Nazareth of Galilee and was baptized by John in the Jordan. And just as he was coming up out of the water, he saw the heavens torn apart and the Spirit descending like a dove on him. And a voice came from heaven, "You are my Son, the Beloved; with you I am well pleased." And the Spirit immediately drove him out into the wilderness. He was in the wilderness forty days, tempted by Satan; and he was with the wild beasts; and the angels waited on him. Now after John was arrested, Jesus came to Galilee, proclaiming the good news of God, and saying, "The time is fulfilled, and the kingdom of God has come near; repent, and believe in the good news."

—MARK 1:9–15

I had the great joy not too long ago to visit with students from Epiphany School in Boston, which began eleven years ago and serves more than eighty kids in fifth through eighth grade who have struggled academically. The school promises they will "never give up on a child." They keep kids in school twelve hours a day, eleven months a year, and they require that the children's families volunteer two hours a week. Three meals are served each school day, and there are cooking classes on Saturday. In order to enter school each day, a child has to shake the hand of the director and look in his eyes. If a kid decides to leave, they keep a space open for him, because those kids almost always come back. They hire young people as teacher interns, and provide them with housing. They've renovated the train stop right outside their door, and they're beginning to think about how to turn an old repair shop next door into housing for students to board during the week and for families in transition. They've developed a conversation with the whole community, and they're transforming the community in the process.

I treasure the times when I get to have a deep and probing conversation with somebody—a conversation that gets beyond superficialities into some real meat, where each of us is changed in the process. Together, the partners in a conversation like that make more of life and thought than either of them could do alone.

Conversation is what Christian community is really meant to be about. The word *conversation* doesn't just mean talking, or at least it didn't when it first began to be used in English around seven hundred years ago. It meant to have dealings with, to be in relationship with. Today, we'd say it means to "hang out." Conversation is what prayer is about, and prayer is far more about spending time with God than it is about using words. Christian community is not about wordplay or debate; it's about encountering each other in a deep enough way to begin to see the image of God in our neighbors.

The word *conversation* has such deep roots in that idea of relationship that in early English usage it was a synonym for the fullest sense of marriage. So much so that there's a legal term in English law, "criminal conversation," a technical term for adultery. It means spending too much time with the wrong person.

The great conversation between God and Noah in the book of Genesis is about re-ordering relationship. After sending a flood that destroys everything on the earth except for one righteous man, Noah, and his family, God says, "Well, maybe I got it wrong. I won't do that again. And I'm so committed to not destroying the world again in a flood that I'll hang up my bow—that thing I use to shoot thunderbolts. That's my covenant, my sign that I will mend this relationship."

Most of the psalms—those songs of joy and sorrow and supplication found in the Hebrew Scriptures—are conversations with God that express the reality of the psalmist's existence. "I'm looking to you, God," they cry, "to keep me safe and dignified and unconquered. Keep teaching me, stay in relationship with me. I need you to remember that you love me, not what I've done wrong."

In the Christian Scriptures, the letter of Peter is about the way that God's relationship with humanity and the rest of creation has again been renewed in Jesus. God's presence among us in Jesus is a conversation that didn't just last a year or three years or even thirty-three years, but continues now and into the future. That conversation goes on day by day, baptism by baptism, holy meal by holy meal, prayer by prayer, and through each encounter, each conversation we have in our daily lives.

We get a glimpse of God's relationship with Jesus in the verbal conversation that takes place at his baptism, as God claims Jesus as beloved son. God calls us beloved as well, and goes further to take pleasure in us, too. It's an astonishing place to start—that God loves us before we do anything, that God loves us just because we are. God calls Jesus beloved before he is driven out into the desert to be tempted, and God calls us beloved before we get a chance to go astray. And our belovedness does not disappear when we mess up or wander off.

God's conversation with us begins before our birth and continues past the grave. That's part of what it means to say that Jesus as the word was with God from the beginning, from before creation (John 1). And it is what it means to say—as Paul did in his letter to the Romans—that nothing can separate us from the love of God, not even death (Romans 8:38–39).

Our job in this conversation is to be God's partners, to respond and receive that good news, to hear it not just with our ears but also with the ear of our heart, as Benedict of Nursia says in his Rule. Our job is to give our hearts to that understanding—that, after all, is what believing means. When Jesus says, "The kingdom of God has come near; repent and believe in the good news" (Mark 1:15), that's exactly what he's talking about. God's in an eternal and blessed conversation with each one of us, so we need to get with the program and act like we've taken it to heart. Repent, turn around, and move back into conscious relationship with God. Strike up that conversation. Take this belovedness into the depths of our being and let it transform us. Then we can begin to live in the world as though we see the other parts of God's creation as equally beloved.

It's not easy. It wasn't easy for Jesus when he headed into the desert right after his baptism. He might have had angels to feed him and wild beasts to keep him company, but his struggle with his own belovedness was not simple or easy. Jesus' encounter with the tempter out there in the desert included a series of apparently simple invitations to end the conversation. One of the ways to wander off, to cut off the conversation, is to believe that our belovedness means that nobody else matters—that we are the center of existence and can use creation for our own ends. That's what Jesus faced, and it's what we face all the time. Ultimately, that's idolatry—it's insisting that God's image can't be found anywhere else. The other way of cutting off the conversation is to deny the truth of our own belovedness—to assume that God really couldn't love us because we're inadequate or hopeless. But that's missing the image of God with which each and every one of us is endowed—it's the same sin of turning away from the image of God, but we've missed that godly reflection in ourselves rather than in others.

Jesus' temptations were not new. They may have been tougher, because he seems to have come to the desert with a strong and deep relational conversation with God already well underway. The cure for our temptations, as for his, is recognizing that the conversation continues, remembering or discovering the presence of God around us and among us and within us, and responding by opening up to the conversation from our end once again.

Conversations don't need a lot of words. A congregation in San Francisco had an unusual Ash Wednesday service recently. They processed half a mile down the street to the exit from a nearby subway station and held their service there on the sidewalk, offering ashes to commuters passing by. Their conversation included a much larger congregation—all those with whom they live, and move, and have their being, even if they don't recognize their interconnectedness most of the time.

How can we get back into the conversation? Spend some time and listen to the voice—"You are my beloved, and in you I am well pleased." Close your eyes, settle in, and hear God saying it to you. Spend a few minutes each morning listening to the voice, and notice how your other conversations change.

For Reflection

Spend some time thinking about prayer as a conversation with God, not just a monologue. Listen deeply for God's voice.

Part Five

Healing Broken Connections

I f God is love, then those who are bound up in God's love can only respond by seeking to expand the scope of belovedness. The search for healing—of human relationships, and between human beings and other parts of creation—in ways we haven't tried or experienced or even imagined before becomes the reason for living, and the ultimate meaning of existence. God is at work—always and everywhere.

Practicing Peace

I therefore, the prisoner in the Lord, beg you to lead a life worthy of the calling to which you have been called, with all humility and gentleness, with patience, bearing with one another in love, making every effort to maintain the unity of the Spirit in the bond of peace. There is one body and one Spirit, just as you were called to the one hope of your calling, one Lord, one faith, one baptism, one God and Father of all, who is above all and through all and in all.

—EPHESIANS 4:1–6

Not too long ago, when I was in Stockton, California, I went running along the river early in the morning, along a bike path—up above the river on a levee on an old railroad grade that let me see the road down below and the yards and parking lots across the way. I passed a school where there were five or six boys skateboarding in the dark. I didn't think much about it, but when I passed by again on my way back, I could hear yelling. Most of these ten- or twelve-year-old boys were still doing skateboard tricks, but one of them was standing in the middle of the court screaming obscenities, as loud as he could in his not-yet-a-man's voice. My initial reaction was irritation at his language, then puzzlement and curiosity. Why were these young boys out by themselves in a dark playground hours before school would start? I began to wonder what I could do, or what anybody could do.

Where did this boy's rage come from? What had his few years brought him, that all he could do was have a tantrum? Why had no one helped him learn how to manage his frustration? And where were the adults in this early-morning darkness?

I kept going, and it struck me that there's a parallel in the church. We have quite a bit of experience dealing with people whose anger is out of control, for the church is one place that will receive you, usually, whatever emotional or spiritual state you're in.

I had a similar experience a few weeks later, on one leg of a flight to Egypt. I'd noticed a well-dressed man who stood out on my way from one terminal to the other. When I arrived at the gate, I walked over near the door to wait for boarding to begin. As soon as the door opened, that well-dressed man rushed up and pushed in front of me, trying to get ahead of the handicapped passengers who were board-ing first. I wasn't terribly surprised to discover that I was assigned the seat next to him. We stowed our things and sat down. The flight attendant came by with newspapers to offer, and this fellow pushed over me to grab one. I very politely asked him not to touch me, and he began to scream and swear at me. So I simply stood up and asked the flight attendant to reseat me.

Where did his rage come from? He certainly looked like he was in charge of the world, and until he lost it, he acted that way, too. But his rage was just as incoherent and inappropriate as that of the boy with the skateboard.

I think both of those guys had lost their way—or perhaps they had never found it. One of the great human yearnings is to have a sense of place, a home where others care for you and make you feel valued and significant. I have to imagine that the boys in the park-ing lot had probably left home or been dropped off because there wasn't anybody to care for or about them at home—maybe parents had to go to work hours before school started, or maybe they just weren't paying attention. The businessman's response to the world was to assume it was all his, to do with as he wished. That does not exactly endear you to the other human beings around you, and it doesn't help build a sense of home for anybody.

The church is meant to be a place where all Jesus' sisters and brothers know they have a home. The scriptural imagery that describes this home is immense, expansive, embracing: the desert will bloom, weak bodies will be made whole, fearful hearts—like the two I encountered—will be made strong, and all creation will rejoice (Isaiah 35:1–10). It's a vision of a world where fear won't keep anybody less than fully human. How do we get there? The letter to the early Christian community in Ephesus has some good suggestions— patience, humility, gentleness, forbearance, and looking for ways to make peace (Ephesians 4:1–6). And the Hebrew prophet Isaiah reminds us that we're not supposed to respond with vengeance, because vengeance is God's, not ours.

There's been a lot of anger and rage in parts of The Episcopal Church in recent years, much of it related to issues of sexuality. Given the stories I've heard in the Dioceses of San Joaquin and Fort Worth, leadership looked a lot like control and fear-mongering, and intimidation was used to keep people in line. Bishops and clergy insisted that they had the fullness of God's truth, and if anybody disagreed, well, then, they must be godless heretics. If nothing else, that's not the way to build a godly unity. It may produce a tight uniformity, like political dictatorships continue to do around the world. But it makes the system ripe for reform or rebellion, because human beings were not created to live in strife—we were created for peace. Isaiah reminds us that that great vision for where we're going is a road to peace and home that is so obvious that even fools won't be able to miss it.

The rage in this world is most often related to missing that road. The job of the church is to help the raging find it. Often that looks like responding to the rage in a counterintuitive way. That is most centrally what Jesus' passion is about. He didn't retaliate, he didn't answer violence with violence, and until his last breath he kept reaching out to his tormentors. Eventually, God's road home became so obvious that even those fearful disciples couldn't miss the reality of resurrection.

I missed a couple of opportunities to try to build a bit more peace in this world. I was too rushed to go down and find out what was wrong in that schoolyard. And I was too tired to find out what was wrong with my seatmate on the plane. It is in refusing to retaliate with violence, and in continually seeking to heal the pain the drives the rage, that our gospel work proceeds.

Episcopalians—and other Christians, too—need to think about where the rage in the wounded places of our churches comes from. At a very basic level, it has to do with some people feeling that there is no home for them in the community they thought was theirs, that they are not valued or welcomed there because they understand something differently, or have a different opinion. The great tragedy is that some believe they will find that home by leaving.

But the reality is that home is found on the road, that road we can't miss because it's so obvious even the silly and the intellectually challenged should be able to find it. It's the road of daily encounters, where we struggle with our fellow skateboarders when they really tick us off, where we make peace with a fellow traveler who has unwittingly made our day more threatening, and where we build communities where kids aren't left alone for hours with no adults to care for them and societies in which men and women can deal with each other as equals. We can even discover that home by reaching out to those who have only been able to find an identity in opposition. God didn't make us for opposition. God made us in all our diversity to figure out how all our differing gifts can bless the world.

The challenge is to remember the joy we already know in relationship each time we have an encounter with the old violence and rage that's part of human systems—in the church and beyond. When we're confronted by rage, our task is to avoid any response that looks like revenge. Acrimony and rage and violence and retribution will not heal the hurt. The only thing that will produce healing is love.

In all the ragged places of our lives, wherever there's anger and hurt and violence, we need to think about how to practice peace. Even if we have to bite our tongue, count to ten, or turn away, we shouldn't get sucked into the spiral of violence. We need to be clear about our identity as kin of the prince of peace, celebrate the gifts that differ, and remember that God has called us together to serve our fellow human beings. In serving our neighbors we will find the road to wholeness, unity, and joy once again.

For Reflection

In times of dissent in your community's life, where have you experienced the practice of peace? How was it manifested?

Pentecost Continues

*When the day of Pentecost had come, they were all together in one
place. And suddenly from heaven there came a sound like the rush of
a violent wind, and it filled the entire house where they were sitting.
Divided tongues as of fire appeared among them, and a tongue rested
on each of them. All of them were filled with the Holy Spirit and
began to speak in other languages as the Spirit gave them ability.*

—ACTS 2:1–4

Christians celebrate the feast of Pentecost as the birthday of the
church. It marks the day when Jesus' apostles—who'd been
hunkered down behind closed doors, afraid to venture out into the
world after his death—received the Holy Spirit, giving them the
courage to spread the gospel. Pentecost, today, is most fundamen-
tally a continuing gift of the spirit—rather than a limitation or
quenching of that spirit—as we continue to seek the courage to
preach the good news we know in Jesus.

Recently, the Archbishop of Canterbury, the spiritual leader of
the Anglican Communion, of which The Episcopal Church is a part,
issued a statement about the struggles within the Communion that
seems to equate Pentecost with a single understanding of gospel
realities. Those who received the gift of the spirit on that day two
thousand years ago all heard good news. The crowd of people who
were there in Jerusalem reported that "in our own languages we hear
them speaking about God's deeds of power" (Acts 2:11).

Today, the spirit does seem to be saying to many within The
Episcopal Church that gay and lesbian persons are God's good creation, that an aspect of good creation is the possibility of lifelong,
faithful partnership, and that such persons may indeed be good and
healthy exemplars of gifted leadership within the church, as baptized leaders and ordained ones. The spirit also seems to be saying
the same thing in other parts of the Anglican Communion, and
among some of our Christian partners, including Lutheran churches
in North America and Europe, the Old Catholic churches of Europe,
and a number of others.

That growing awareness does not deny the reality that many
Anglicans and not a few Episcopalians still fervently hold traditional
views about human sexuality. This Episcopal Church is a broad and
inclusive enough tent to hold that variety. The willingness to live in
tension is a hallmark of Anglicanism, beginning from its roots in
Celtic Christianity pushing up against Roman Christianity in the
centuries of the first millennium. That diversity in community was
solidified in the Elizabethan Settlement—the legislation that
reestablished Protestantism in England during the reign of Queen
Elizabeth I, while retaining many "Catholic" traditions, such as vest-
ments and saints' days. The Elizabethan Settlement really marks the
beginning of Anglican Christianity as a distinct movement. Above
all, it recognizes that the spirit may be speaking to all of us, in ways
that do not at present seem to cohere or agree. It also recognizes
what Jesus says about the spirit to his followers, "I still have many
things to say to you, but you cannot bear them now. When the spirit
of truth comes, he will guide you into all the truth; for he will not
speak on his own, but will speak whatever he hears, and he will
declare to you the things that are to come" (John 16:12–13).

The Episcopal Church has spent nearly fifty years listening to
and for the spirit in these matters. While it is clear that not all within
this church have heard the same message, the current developments
do represent a widening understanding. Our church laws reflected

this shift as long ago as 1985, when sexual orientation was first protected from discrimination in access to the process for ordination of
clergy. At the request of other bodies in the Anglican Communion,
this church held an effective moratorium on the election and consecration of partnered gay or lesbian priests as bishops from 2003 to
2010. When the Diocese of Los Angeles elected such a person,
Mary Glasspool, in late 2009, the ensuing consent process indicated
that a majority of the laity, clergy, and bishops responsible for vali-
dating that election agreed that there was no substantive bar to her
consecration as a suffragan bishop in the Diocese of Los Angeles.

The Episcopal Church recognizes that these decisions are prob-
lematic to a number of other Anglicans. We have not made these
decisions lightly. We recognize that the spirit has not been widely
heard in the same way in other parts of the Communion. In all
humility, we recognize that we may be wrong, yet we have pro-
ceeded in the belief that the spirit permeates our decisions.

We also recognize that the attempts to impose a singular understanding in such matters represent the same kind of cultural excesses
practiced by many of our colonial forebears in their missionizing
activity. Native Hawaiians were forced to abandon their traditional
dress in favor of missionaries' standards of modesty. Native Americans
were forced to abandon many of their cultural practices, even though
they were fully congruent with orthodox Christianity, because the missionaries did not understand those practices or consider them to be
exemplary of the spirit. The uniformity imposed at the Synod of Whitby
in 663 did similar violence to a developing, contextual Christianity
in the British Isles, as Roman traditions were imposed in place of the
unique traditions of Celtic Christianity that had flourished for centuries
in Britain. In their search for uniformity, our forebears in the faith have
repeatedly done much spiritual violence in the name of Christianity.

We do not seek to impose our understanding on others. We do
earnestly hope for continued dialogue with those who disagree, for
we believe that the spirit is always calling us to greater understanding.

We live in great concern, however, that colonial attitudes continue, particularly in attempts to impose a single understanding across widely varying contexts and cultures. We note that the cultural contexts in which The Episcopal Church's decisions have generated the greatest objection and reaction are also often the same contexts where women are barred from full ordained leadership, including the Church of England (which still does not permit women to serve as bishops).

As Episcopalians, we note the troubling push toward centralized authority exemplified in many of the Archbishop of Canterbury's recent statements. Anglicanism as a body began in the repudiation of the control of the Bishop of Rome within the otherwise sovereign nation of England. Similar concerns over self-determination in the face of colonial control led the Church of Scotland to consecrate Samuel Seabury in 1784 as the first bishop of The Episcopal Church in the nascent United States—and so began the Anglican Communion.

The Episcopal Church has been repeatedly assured that the Anglican Covenant—a proposed document that would commit individual Anglican churches to consult the wider Communion when making major decisions—is not an instrument of control. Yet we note that the fourth section seems to be just that to Anglicans in many parts of the Communion. So much so that there are voices calling for stronger sanctions in that fourth section, as well as voices repudiating it as un-Anglican in nature. Unitary control does not characterize Anglicanism; rather, diversity in fellowship and communion does.

We in The Episcopal Church are distressed at the apparent imposition of sanctions on some parts of the Communion. We note that these seem to be limited to those that "have *formally*, through their Synod or House of Bishops"—their churchwide governing bodies—"adopted policies that breach any of the moratoria requested by the Instruments of Communion." We are further distressed that such sanctions do not, apparently, apply to those parts of the Communion that continue to hold one view in public and exhibit other behaviors in private—a wink and a nod to things that go on but are not publicly recognized—such as partnered same-sex clergy in the Church of England. Why is there no sanction on those who continue with a double standard? In our context, bowing to anxiety by ignoring that sort of double-mindedness is usually termed a "failure of nerve." Through many decades of wrestling with our own discomfort about recognizing the full humanity of persons who seem to differ from us, we continue to work at open and transparent communication as well as congruence between word and behavior. We openly admit our failure to achieve perfection.

The baptismal covenant prayed in The Episcopal Church for more than thirty years calls us to respect the dignity of all other persons and charges us with ongoing labor toward a holy society of justice and peace. That fundamental understanding of Christian vocation underlies our hearing of the spirit in this context and around these issues of human sexuality. That same understanding of Christian vocation encourages us to hold our convictions with sufficient humility that we can affirm the image of God in the person who disagrees with us. We believe that the body of Christ—the Church—is only found when such diversity is welcomed with abundant and radical hospitality.

As a church of many nations, languages, and peoples, Episcopalians will continue to seek every opportunity to increase our partnership in God's mission for a healed creation and holy community. We look forward to the ongoing growth in partnership possible in the Listening Process, Continuing Indaba, Bible in the Life of the Church, Theological Education in the Anglican Communion, and the myriad less formal and more local partnerships across the Communion—all of them efforts to allow clergy and laypeople the chance to hear the faith stories of Christians whose lives and understandings are different from their own. These are experiences of conversation about mission and ministry that inform and transform individuals and communities toward the vision of the gospel—a healed world, loving God and neighbor, in the love and friendship shown us in God Incarnate.

For Reflection

Consider the faith stories of those whose beliefs are different from yours. What can you learn from them about a healed world?

Living the Questions

I do not call you servants any longer, because the servant does not know what the master is doing; but I have called you friends.

—JOHN 15:1

A while ago, I visited a diocese that's reorganizing after many of their leaders left The Episcopal Church, and the people there peppered me with questions. The questions were fascinating, and somewhat different than the ones I hear in dioceses that are closer to the mainstream in the Episcopal Church. "If it's OK for New Hampshire to elect a gay bishop," one person demanded, "why isn't it right for the church to accept a bishop who believes that women shouldn't be ordained?"

We started with the canons—the laws that govern the activities of the church—and the expectation that dioceses provide access to the discernment process for women, even if the bishop is unwilling to ordain women himself. That led us into a conversation about discernment for ordained ministry, and the ways in which discernment is a mutual conversation between the individual and the wider community. It's clear that not everyone should be ordained, but it should be equally clear that every baptized person is meant to be involved in ministry. If we asked vocational questions of all the faithful, and did the discernment work as carefully with all our members, we would have fewer questions and fights over discernment to ordained ministry.

Ordination, of course, means limitation. I can't do things as the Presiding Bishop of The Episcopal Church that I did as the Bishop of Nevada, and I couldn't do things as Bishop of Nevada that I did as a parish priest in Oregon, and I couldn't do things as a parish priest in Oregon that I did as a layperson. Here's an example: I visited the Diocese of Vermont shortly after the House of Bishops of The Episcopal Church had agreed to a common understanding of a request that the Anglican Communion had made of our church when they asked us to refrain from consecrating new bishops whose "manner of life" offered a challenge to the wider Communion. The people the Anglican Communion officials were talking about, we opined, were partnered gay and lesbian persons.

The clergy in Vermont were livid about this request. "You know, when I was bishop of Nevada," I said to them, "my responsibility was to a different group of people than it is now. I'm supposed to be pastor to the whole church, and that includes people who are certain that Bishop Gene Robinson should be bishop of New Hampshire and people who are certain he should never have been ordained. I may not agree with all of them, but my task is to provide pastoral care—or see that it is provided—for all the people in this church."

Each time we say yes to serving, it involves a diminishment, a lessening of some kinds of freedom. Where does most of our ministry take place? Baptismal ministry—and every single Christian is a minister by virtue of his or her baptism—takes place mostly out there in daily life, in the world. Deacons have much greater access to the wider community than most parish priests do; their primary responsibility is the community beyond the church walls, while most priests' responsibility is primarily within the congregational community. Bishops are in the awkward place of pastoring the clergy as well as accepting a pastoral responsibility for the community beyond the church, in a less hands-on and more systemic way than most deacons do.

That kind of limitation is at least part of what the prayer is pointing toward when it says, "Grant us so to glory in the cross that we gladly suffer shame and loss."[1] We have accepted a loss and limitation for the sake of the gospel. Part of that loss has to be a willingness to surrender the ministry of leadership to others in the community. The much-distressed dioceses of The Episcopal Church where former leaders have voted to leave The Episcopal Church have given us clear examples of how possessive leadership leads to dysfunction. Ordained leadership is supposed to be kenotic—the kind of self-emptying that God did in becoming human—and so is the ministry of every baptized person. We're all supposed to give ministry away, build it up in others, and get ourselves off center stage. That does look shameful in the world's eyes.

That kind of shame and loss is what Jesus is talking about when he says you have to die to bear fruit, and you have to lose your life in order to save it, and hate it to keep it for eternity (Matthew 10:39). We're asked to be servants, at the service of the hungry and needy—but servants who work for transformation, not servants who coddle dysfunction and dependence. Jesus is somebody who serves, feeds, heals; who teaches, equips, and challenges others; who gives power away—and who at the last surrenders even life itself.

And in that surrender is the abundance of life for which we were created and redeemed. That surrender frees us to discover that our territory is the whole world, and we don't need to possess it, for God has given us that garden as a field ready for harvest.

Think about the way in which we specify those losses and shames, those ordered spheres of ministry, when we examine a candidate for baptism or for ordained ministry.

The deacon is challenged to "serve all people, particularly the poor, the weak, the sick, and the lonely" and "seek not your glory but the glory of the Lord Christ."

The priest is challenged to "love and serve the people among whom you work" and "offer all your labors to God."

The bishop is reminded to "encourage and support all baptized people in their gifts and ministries," "to be merciful to all, show compassion to poor and strangers, and defend those who have no helper," and "to follow him who came not to be served but to serve, and to give his life as ransom for many."

All of these are rooted in the challenge that is offered to each and every person who is baptized: "Will you continue in the apostles' teaching and fellowship, persevere in resisting evil, seek and serve Christ in all persons, proclaim good news by word and example, and strive for justice among all people?"

My adult spiritual journey began with the death of a childhood friend. It led me back to a church community to wrestle with the loss. My inability to continue as an oceanographer in my early thirties was a profound shame—suddenly I had lost my identity and the dream I'd worked toward for many years. Beginning the journey toward ordination was an acknowledgment that that dream was finally dead. When I graduated from seminary, I had three part-time offers of employment, two of them ninety miles away from my family. I chose the one in the community that had nurtured my priestly vocation. Before long, I had to attend the institution of a friend and classmate as rector. For a while, I felt shamed that I hadn't lived up to that standard somebody else had set. But I began to discover that part-time ministry in the parish gave me at once the opportunity to learn the discipline of managing time, the ability to say yes to other ministries such as teaching at the university and being a hospice chaplain, and the ability to challenge the workaholic rector who used to say that he was the most responsible person he knew. I'm still trying to find the balance between servanthood and overfunctioning—one is grace and blessing, the other sin and selfishness, and indeed the opposite of kenotic leadership.

As ministers of the gospel—for indeed, that's what each of us is—we're supposed to be willing to acknowledge the ways in which loss and shame have shown us the glory of servanthood. Discovering how shame and loss become gifts is an essential part of discernment, and discernment is what keeps us moving and growing as faithful ministers of the gospel.

For Reflection

Where have you discovered shame or loss becoming a blessing?

High Anxiety

Then Jesus said to them, "Do not be afraid. Go and tell my broth-ers to go to Galilee; there they will see me."

—MATTHEW 28:10

In the Christian Scriptures, just about every time the resurrected Jesus appears, his disciples respond with fear and anxiety. Each gospel tells about the encounters at Jesus' tomb using the language of fear. In Matthew, the guards are paralyzed by fear (Matthew 28:4); the women respond in fear when they discover the tomb empty or when they meet the angels (Matthew 28:8). The Marys try to hang on to him (Matthew 28:9–10), and so do Cleopas and his friend on the road to Emmaus (Luke 24:18). After their fellow traveler begins to explain what's been going on, they absolutely insist that he stay with them. The disciples in the upper room are terrified when Jesus gets past the locked doors (John 20:26). And even in the scene on the shore of the Sea of Galilee, when Jesus meets the guys who've gone back to fishing, and then cooks them a meal from their catch, they don't quite have the courage to ask him who he is (John 21:9–13). Even when they're not consumed with fear and trembling, they all can't quite believe he is who they think he is—every single one of them, not just Thomas, is uncertain.

Why do people always seem to get anxious when Jesus turns up? It happens all through his ministry. He turns up in the temple and the

177

authorities get nervous. He turns up in Jerusalem and the Romans arrest and execute him.

Jesus still makes people nervous. That fear and anxiety is what got Oscar Romero shot, for standing up for the oppressed in El Salvador, and Martin Luther King Jr., for advocating for African Americans in the United States, and Dorothy Stang, for working for the poor in Brazil.

We're dealing with much lower level anxieties in ecumenical circles, but they've got the same roots. Why can't the Episcopalians and the Baptists and Presbyterians all just get along? It's probably because each of us is territorial about Jesus. Most of us think we have a monopoly on how to understand him, and worship him, and imitate him. And most of us get a bit nervous when he really does show up and give evidence of his presence in other people and other communities, and in ways that simply don't fit with how *we* have always done things.

As Lent began a couple of years ago, I attended a gathering of representatives of the churches involved in Churches Uniting in Christ (CUIC). We came together on Ash Wednesday to figure out if there was any life left in that body, or if we should just give CUIC a decent burial. That endeavor had been moribund for several years because of actions that some deemed offensive, even racist. In the last two years I had come to understand that the wound had something to do with the action of an Episcopalian—for which I tried to apologize to some of those who had been offended. That attempt was rejected, and then met with a profound urge toward healing and reconciliation. One person said, "Today is today and yesterday was yesterday. We're not going to dwell on the past. I'm here to see if we can get this body moving again. It's time for all of us to grow up a little more and recognize that when we disagree it's not necessarily because of racism." We spent much of Ash Wednesday trying to discover how these seeds of new life might begin to take root and flourish.

The decisions that came out of that resurrection meeting led us toward joint work on ending racism in our churches and the larger society, and figuring out how to work together to relieve the suffering of Haitians, both here in the United States and in their native land. We closed our meeting with a communion service, jointly celebrated by four bishops of the Methodist tradition: United Methodist, African Methodist Episcopal, Christian Methodist Episcopal, and African Methodist Episcopal Zion. And though some liturgists would tremble or fume at such a practice during a somber observance of Ash Wednesday, we sang *alleluia* with great vigor!

Fear and anxiety can keep us locked up in our various and separated rooms. But Jesus sneaks in anyway.

Those of us who work to heal division among the branches of Christianity must deal with those fears, small and large, and invite Jesus in, through the open doors of our hearts, to be touched and seen in unexpected ways. Most of us aren't quite going to believe it, but he's here, and well beyond here, continuing to challenge us to live in peace rather than fear.

The sacramental experience of eating and serving together is always the place to find Jesus, whether it's a fish barbecue on the beach, building homes in New Orleans, lobbying Washington on behalf of Haiti, or meeting with those of other faith traditions to find mutual understanding.

When we work on ecumenical issues, we may experience the eternal tension between what some see as primary about right Christian belief and what others prioritize as good solid Christian action—orthodoxy and orthopraxy—or even the old split between "faith and order" and "life and work." That tension can either be a lock on the door and a refusal to recognize Jesus in our midst, or it can be a reminder to welcome the crucified one.

Will we welcome the crucified one by noting that he died only for us? Or will we really look at that cross? It's made up of right angles—what mathematicians call orthogonals. We know that God's geometry can move beyond the predictability of orthogonals—and beyond orthodoxy and orthopraxy. That tension is resolved in resurrection, where God is doing something beyond what any of us can predict or imagine. Our divisions recede, and are transformed in the encounter with the risen one.

There's another term mathematicians use for those right angles—the technical term for two lines or planes that intersect at a right angle is "normal." There is a great tendency in ecumenical conversations to assume that there's only one "normal," and that it's our preferred way of understanding Jesus or engaging the world. God's geometry has many angles, though, and all of them can be in right relationship to God, even if they don't seem to be normal to us. If God is beyond our imagining, then there must be many normal, right relationships with God that are also beyond our imagining. We are, after all, talking about the eternal hyperspace as well as three dimensions.

Our task is to move beyond the normal and predictable, to a kind of hope beyond imagining. Our challenge is to hope with the kind of wild abandon that expects to find resurrection in spite of the world's focus on morbidity and normality.

Our job is to hope for God's commonwealth here on earth, and insist that it come speedily. Working together as people of faith, pushing beyond the paralysis of fear, we can move toward a world with no more abused children, no more war-torn nations, no more neglected and ignored human beings on our doorsteps, no more lives without access to the abundance for which each was created, no more of God's children who can't go to school or find meaningful employment. Together we can move toward healing and restoring creation to the garden it was meant to be, that it might support God's children in abundance, and that there may be marvelous catches of fish to feed them, for eons yet to come. May that be the true normal.

We can hope for that, if we'll let go of the fear. The next time Jesus turns up, don't get anxious—get busy. Things will go a lot better, moving together toward a new normal as followers of Jesus.

For Reflection

Consider the ways that fear plays a part in contentious relationships. Make a practice of reminding yourself of the words of the divine messengers to "fear not."

Pushing the Boundaries

*For I am about to create new heavens and a new earth; the former
things shall not be remembered or come to mind.*

—Isaiah 65:17

A while back, I spent several days with a ten-year-old boy, the grandson of my father's wife. I hadn't seen him since he was four or five and I was astonished to see that he had been growing like crazy and was eating half a dozen times a day. Most of the time he was off running to the beach and jumping in the pool and doing a pretty good job of entertaining himself. A lot of the time he was listening to books on his iPod, wearing big stereo headphones. I tried repeatedly to engage him in conversation, without much success, until I remembered that most ten-year-olds don't have long conversations. He wasn't mischievous or misbehaved, but he was exceedingly energetic, and his parents assured me that he didn't need constant supervision.

In a year or two I could see him doing just what Jesus did, and deciding that heading out to explore was far more enticing than staying home with the parental units. Jesus the child, congruent with the adult, acts in unexpected and nontraditional ways—at least from his parents' perspective. One gospel account tells us that he goes off to the Temple to ask questions and to listen. He doesn't ask permission, and when his parents find him, he doesn't ask forgiveness. But he seems to know that he's doing what he's supposed to be doing (Luke 2:39–50).

Let's put ourselves in Joseph's shoes. Jesus' "foster father" had already managed to let go of his own control needs when confronted with Mary's unanticipated pregnancy and the pending birth of this child. He'd done either the foolish thing or the noble or holy thing and accepted the child as his own. And it's apparent that this child isn't exactly what he expected—later on, as an adult, the family all think he's crazy (Mark 3:21). But here in Jerusalem, that child apparently doesn't have any compunction about transgressing his parents' agenda. What do you do with somebody who keeps pushing the boundaries?

Yet the evidence mounts up in the gospels that this is exactly what Jesus is about. His continual message, his constant work, is pushing the boundaries and crossing the limits that separate us from the reign of God. Love all your neighbors, he insists, even the ones who hate you—including those half-breed, heretic Samaritans, despised by first-century Jews. Healing is more important than rules about what work is permitted on the Sabbath. Purity and acceptability are not part of the invitation to God's table.

Paul the Apostle understands that, when he notes that God's promise to Abraham didn't come through the law, but through right relationship. Grace and blessing are the fruit of vulnerability to God's work in us, around us, through us. And if we stick it out, that faithful relationship will keep on confronting us with continuing creation, courtesy of the God "who gives life to the dead and calls into existence the things that do not exist" (Romans 4:17). Joseph discovered that repeatedly—in coping with an unexpected pregnancy, in sheltering this new life from the evil of the world that would destroy it, in living with a child who grew up in unexpected ways. Jesus' life and ministry are all about the God who calls into existence things that don't yet exist. The reign of God doesn't yet exist in its fullness, but we insist that's where we're going.

The Episcopal Church today—like many other Christian communities—is waiting to see what will emerge in a church that

doesn't yet exist. We are eagerly expectant to see how we can partner in that emergence.

What seem to be emerging are new forms of Christian community—or maybe better, new aspects of Christian community. Often,
leaders of these new communities are reluctant to let their stories be
told more broadly because they're afraid of their religious institutions. They're afraid of what their bishops will do with lay and
clergy leaders who are pushing the boundaries.

But do we profess to believe in the God who gives life to the
dead—including the moribund parts of the church? Do we really
believe that God is calling into existence things that don't yet exist?
Or are we going to retreat to the laws and the traditions? That's not
where new life emerges. That's not where the promises of new life
are met and fulfilled.

Joseph had the courage to risk a great deal of what he knew and
found comfort in, for the sake of the new things God was up to. Do
we have the courage to risk thinking and acting in new ways?

An essential part of growing up, either into adulthood or the full
stature of Jesus, is about learning courage, learning from risk and
failure, and discovering that there is new life in the face of all sorts
of death. The parents of my ten-year-old friend have the courage to
let him run around exploring new things. Do we as Christians have
the courage to risk new ways?

I don't believe that either Joseph or Jesus was lawless. I do
believe each had the kind of relationship with God that helped tran-
scend their fears, and transmute them, so that the word of the law,
its life-giving spirit, could be released to bring into existence things
that did not yet exist. For leaders in the church, that is equally the
charge. We cannot take refuge in an ironclad tradition that sucks the
life out of the living body, nor ignore the guides and limits that mark
a healthy community. For Episcopalians, the challenge and opportunity in this age is to hold the tension between the two, and find
some traditionally novel Anglican middle way.

It is abundantly clear that many of the old ways of presenting the gospel in our age have failed. They have failed because they don't take seriously the ways in which God is already at work around us. God is already bringing into existence kinds of Christian communities that have not existed before, at least not in our memory—and somehow, that renewal always seems to come from the edges. The evangelical renewal taking place in Africa is one kind, which as it grows is pushing the boundaries of a former center in Western Christianity. At the same time there is new life emerging in those contexts we inhabit. The bishop of Haiti tells us that his church is growing in the aftermath of the earthquake because it is showing God's love for all who turn up. Faith communities tend to grow when they get beyond self-preservation and focus instead on the needs of others.

Some of these new and edgy communities may send traditionalists screaming into the night. While not all of them are examples to be emulated, there is abundant evidence that God is at work in those places where God has always been at work, bringing new life out of old—in prisons, on the streets and under the bridges of our cities, in communities where young adults are asking eternal questions, in the military, on Indian reservations, wherever people know that they themselves are not the center of the world.

Do we have the courage to follow Jesus in new ways? Are we willing to be like the twelve-year-old in the temple, listening and asking questions? It's not worth doing unless we're willing to discover something new about our vocation. That can be frightening, and will likely involve dying to some old ideas or ways of doing things. Yet that's where God is giving life to the dead and bringing into existence things that do not yet exist. Our job as a church is to stay and engage the questions, to keep pushing the boundaries and to always remain open to the new things that God has in store for us.

For Reflection

Consider the child Jesus in the temple, asking obnoxious questions. What might the adult Jesus be talking about when he says you have to be like a child to enter the kingdom of heaven?

Go Forth for God

Go forth for God, go to the world in peace;
Be of good courage, armed with heavenly grace
In God's good spirit daily to increase
Til in his kingdom we behold his face.

—J.R. PEACEY (1896–1971)

In a few places, The Episcopal Church is growing. In 2009, four United States dioceses grew both in average worship attendance and in baptized membership: Navajoland, North Dakota, Wyoming, and Alabama. Most of our overseas dioceses are growing numerically. The rest, however, are shrinking, either slightly or precipitously.

There are lots of reasons why this is happening. It's not primarily about theological differences, for we grew slightly in the late 1990s and our differences of opinion aren't significantly different ten years later. The decline began about the year 2000, well before the election of the church's first openly gay bishop in New Hampshire. Although conflict in the church doesn't help us grow, that's only a small part of the story.

There *are* cultural components—even in the Bible Belt, there is no longer the assumption and expectation that everyone is in church on Sunday morning. Soccer games, Starbucks, and lots of other things attract people then. The fastest growing religious affiliation in the United States is "none of the above," including 16 percent of all adults and a quarter of eighteen- to twenty-nine-year-olds. One-quarter of young adult Americans have no religious affiliation.

For a long time, The Episcopal Church depended on evangelism by reproduction. We brought new Episcopalians with us when we came to church—they were our children. With the average Episcopalian now fifty-seven years old, we're not bringing so many little ones anymore. The average American is thirty-seven, which may begin to give an idea of how skewed our population is.

Episcopalians have long expected others to come and join us, so we have never learned to do active evangelism very well. Most of us didn't see the need—with the exception of those in the evangelical wing of this church, who have always understood the urgency. That part of the church has always found it hardest to stay in the diverse Anglican fold—maybe because the rest don't always understand the urgency.

The Episcopal Church *can* grow, however—and the statistics back that up. We did grow in the late 1990s, when other mainline denominations were declining. We're growing in immigrant communities and overseas dioceses. The reality is that the church of this century is likely to look quite different from the church of fifty years ago or even fifteen years ago. For one thing, it will be far less white—the fields are ripe for harvest, but not necessarily white for harvest. This church is 87 percent white, 6 percent African American, 3 percent Latino, 1 percent Asian, 1 percent Native American—the United States part of the church, that is. The U.S. population, however, is significantly more diverse (two-thirds non-Latino white, 13 percent African American, 15 percent Latino, 4 percent Asian, and 1 percent Native American). Native Americans are the only group represented at the same rate in The Episcopal Church as in the larger population. All other non-white populations are significantly underrepresented.

Yet that ancient hymn has long charged us to "go forth for God"—not to sit in the pews and wait for people to turn up. God tells Abraham to "go from your country and your kindred and your father's house to the land that I will show you" (Genesis 12:1). "Leave home!" God tells us, too. We have to be willing to leave our lovely churches, to walk out our beautiful red doors, and discover God already at work in the larger community. We're meant to go forth and get to work—in campus ministry, prison ministry—wherever we encounter a need.

A dozen or so young adults, both women and men, are part of the youth delegation to the United Nations Commission on the Status of Women, which meets in New York every winter. They ask wonderful questions about how to improve the lives of women and how to ensure women's reproductive rights. They talk about the effects of wars on women and about war in general. They talk about what to focus on here in the U.S., and about how the church can be a support for gay, lesbian, and transgendered people, and about a whole raft of other things.

When I met with them recently and asked what they would want the larger church to know about them and their peers, they said things such as, "We're passionate; we value and want to be in relationship with our elders; we are not just interested in technical communication like Facebook and texting—we want face-to-face relationships; we are Episcopalians because we find Episcopal spirituality fits us best, and we need more flexibility in worship." Many of them have become Episcopalians very recently, either by baptism or by conversion from another tradition. They are idealistic and urgently interested in changing the world. Yet almost no one will meet them—or other passionate, involved young men and women like them—by staying home.

If we really want to follow Jesus, we *are* going to have to leave home. That's a good part of what he means by saying, "Pick up your cross and follow me" in Luke 9:23. It doesn't just mean we're going to have to suffer. It means that we have to get on the road, see new territory, and experience God in new situations. It means we have to leave our comfortably padded pews. It means we must pick up our cross and see the world—from a new perspective. Imagine Jesus as a travel agent or tour guide who wants to lead us into new places.

One of the more effective evangelical tools right now does just that—it goes into the places where people spend time, at work and at leisure, and it gathers people who want to ask significant spiritual questions. Asking questions is actually something that sets Episcopalians apart from a lot of other traditions, particularly the ones who say there's only one right answer and doubt is a sin. Asking questions is a central part of our tradition. We don't insist that doubt is a sin; we see doubt as necessary to growth.

Young people are hard-wired to ask questions: *Why?* is the most characteristic word out of the mouth of a healthy developing child. *Why should I do that? Why is the stove hot? Why aren't girls and boys always treated the same? Why are some people poor? Why has your generation left the world in such a mess? Why is it so hard to bring peace to the world?* When we stop asking questions like that we begin to die—spiritually, intellectually, emotionally, and probably physically, too.

Building communities where young people can ask the really big questions is one of the most important kinds of evangelism we can do—and the other important kinds of evangelism are about building communities where others can do the same thing. "Theology on Tap" is a prime example—it offers welcome and hospitality, including a brew (caffeinated or spirited), conversation, and community. It is happening in bars, in coffeehouses—wherever people gather. There are many other ways to gather questioners, some of them focused on faith in the workplace. We have always gathered to ask questions. The traditional women's guilds and men's guilds in the church did similar work, but they expected people to show up in the church building. Today we need to go out into the world to provide hospitable places for questioners.

One of the most powerful witnesses to going forth is the recent activity in Haiti. During the January 2010 earthquake, almost all the

Diocese of Haiti's church buildings in Port-au-Prince were destroyed. The people of the diocese are ministering to their members and their neighbors in the open air, offering hospitality to all comers. They haven't just been sent forth, they've been propelled, shaken out of their homes and churches. "Despite the difficulties we face," Bishop Jean Zaché Duracin of Haiti wrote in a letter, "many of our parishes have grown larger since the earthquake, because more and more people trust our church and are turning to us for help spiritually, socially, and morally."

Leading a faithful life means taking up our cross and following Jesus down the road. There are an awful lot of people out there who need an opportunity to ask important questions—young adults, Spanish speakers, Chinese and Russian immigrants, and many people who need to know they are loved whether they ask questions or not. We have something very important to offer all of them. Hardly anyone is too old or too young to go out there and offer that kind of love and hospitality. Are we ready to go out on the road?

Going forth, getting on the road again, is a path to new life for us and for our faith communities. Otherwise, we die.

For Reflection

Think of the unexpected roads you've traveled. What did those journeys teach you?

Fossils

A new heart I will give you, and a new spirit I will put within you; and I will remove from your body the heart of stone and give you a heart of flesh.

— Ezekiel 36:26

More than 135 years ago, Father Charles Quintard—who later became the first Episcopal bishop of Tennessee—challenged the people of his parish to think boldly and build bigger so they could serve a larger community. He urged them to be aggressive in "shaking off this fossilism." What a wonderfully rich image! He clearly envisioned overturning the limits on living a Christian life.

Fossilism has something to do with what the Hebrew prophets call a heart of stone—a heart unmoved by the lament of God's people or the call of God's spirit. Fossilism is a chronic hazard in the church. Frozen in time, sealed in amber, we tend to dream too small or have too narrow a view of where God is calling us. As Jaroslav Pelikan, scholar of religion and author of the 1984 book *The Vindication of Tradition*, says,

> Tradition is the living faith of the dead; traditionalism is the dead faith of the living. Tradition lives in conversation with the past, while remembering where we are and when we are and that it is we who have to decide. Traditionalism supposes that nothing should ever be

> done for the first time, so all that is needed to solve any
> problem is to arrive at the supposedly unanimous testi-
> mony of this homogenized tradition.[1]

In active, engaged, gospel-driven faith communities, though, fossilism doesn't have much chance to settle in—their faith reminds them
of the breath of God enlivening everyone. That warm breath turns
fossils into living flesh, ready for partnership in God's mission.

And mission, after all, is the raison d'être of Christians. Emil
Brunner, a renowned twentieth-century Swiss theologian, put it this
way: "The church exists by mission as a fire exists by burning." That
fire warms cold and weary bones as they join in God's labor, healing
and restoring creation.

The Hebrew prophet Zechariah invites us to dream about a city
where the streets are safe enough for elders to sit sunning themselves
on benches, while little children play around their feet. And not just
to dream about it, but to begin to work toward it, to let those fos-
silized bones live, to make real God's intent for us all. Hear the word
of the Lord, he says: "For there shall be a sowing of peace; the vine
shall yield its fruit, the ground shall give its produce, and the skies
shall give their dew; and I will cause the remnant of this people to
possess all these things" (Zechariah 8:12).

That remnant is old bones that have begun to fossilize, out of
fear or hopelessness or the absence of imagination. Can you imagine
a city where all children have several interested adults ensuring that
they live up to God's dream for them? Can you imagine a city where
it's safe for old ladies and little children to walk down the street at
midnight? Can you imagine a city where nobody has to sleep under
a bridge? Where each and every human person has an opportunity
to put his or her gifts to work in creative and dignified ways? Can
you imagine that?

Imagination—call it dreaming or creative possibility—is one of
the ways we reflect the image of God. The words *image* and *imagine*

come from the Latin *imitatio*, which also gives us the word *imitate*. When we live into the image of God we mirror or imitate God's qualities. That's what Thomas à Kempis was getting at in his spiritual classic *The Imitation of Christ*. And when we turn away from God's possibility because we just can't imagine it, we actually commit sin. God is always up to more than we can imagine. And the world is always pushing back: "Incarnation?" the world asks derisively. "No way!" "Resurrection—not in my frame of reference." "Free the slaves? No, God intended slavery. Here's where it says so in the Bible."

But the imagination of prophets is always nudging or prodding us to open a little wider and let the breath of God blow in. It can be frightening and painful to endure that stretching, but the promise is always this: God is with us.

That's what goes on with Bartimaeus, the blind man in the gospel story who calls out to Jesus. Jesus' response gives him the courage to claim the boldest possibility he can imagine—seeing again. Jesus tells him, "Go, your faith, your willingness to imagine, has made you well and whole." That's Bartimaeus' sending, his commissioning. He heard those words, got up, and "followed Jesus on the way" (Mark 10:52).

Following Jesus on the way is about imagining that healed world that moves beyond dead fossils. Christians have done that throughout our history: Consider Francis of Assisi, who challenged the social order of fifteenth-century Europe, or Desmond Tutu, who stood up to the forces that tried to keep apartheid in place in South Africa. Consider all the saints in our midst who have imagined a faithful community that will look very different from "the way we've always done things." Our challenge as Christians is to follow Jesus on the way that leads out the door, which may be the hardest thing of all.

Our task is to keep imagining a future that looks more like the reign of God. We will need both the prophets who can speak the vision into concrete words and the quieter prophets who read to children and feed the hungry. We will need some who will speak

God's truth in tight places, such as city councils and state legislatures and even ecumenical gatherings, inviting people to stretch their collective imagination and build a society that reflects the divine. We can encourage prophets like the one I read about recently who teaches business skills in the poorest communities in India. He said one abused woman wouldn't even lift her head and look him in the face when he began his class, but that before long she left an abusive marriage, sued for child support, and started a grocery store. She wants to go to law school so she can work with other abused women. She is finding imagination.

And in all the imagining work, we need the nurture of the mystics such as Thomas à Kempis and the pastoral leaders in our parishes and communities, who keep calling us back to prayer. That's where the warm, moist breath enters, the breath that turns fossilizing bones into flesh-covered ones. As a church, if we're willing to be bold, creative, brave, and faithful, we will indeed bless many.

For Reflection

Where is God's image becoming flesh within our church? What can we imagine about God's possibility? How is the great dream becoming flesh and blood reality?

A Moveable Feast

People will come from east and west and north and south, and will take their places at the feast in the kingdom of God.

— LUKE 13:29 (NIV)

I come from a notorious place—the city of Las Vegas. Gambling and prostitution are legal in Nevada, and ministry there means that many congregations host twelve-step programs not just for alcoholics and drug addicts but also for those addicted to gambling. There are a few groups for sex addicts, too. A story quietly circulated when I was bishop there, about a priest who encouraged the local madams and their employees to visit the churches he served. One congregation made a warm enough welcome that the women of the night returned frequently. Other congregations acted more like Jesus' fellow dinner guests did when a woman of ill repute showed up, as told in Luke 7:36–50: "Who let *her* in here?" The women didn't return to those dinner tables.

In some circles The Episcopal Church has the reputation for being a place where you have to dress correctly and know how to act—you really *should* know all the responses in the worship services by heart, and be able to find your way around the several books we use in worship—or you shouldn't even bother walking in the front door. I'll admit that there are a few places like that, where the local pew-sitters are more afraid than their potential guests, but there are lots more communities where all comers are not just invited, but welcomed with open arms.

I have an old friend, a quirky priest who's been a college chaplain for decades, who tells about the summer he traveled across the United States visiting different churches. He was camping, and didn't get a bath every day, but he talked about what a different reception he'd get when he wore his collar, even when he was grubby. The bishop of Rhode Island spent part of her last sabbatical learning what it's like to live on the street. She tells about sleeping in homeless shelters in some of her own churches, and then going upstairs to church on Sunday morning. She was never recognized, but she learned a great deal about the welcome and unwelcome of different congregations.

It's hard work to get to the point where you're able and willing to see the Lord of love in the odorous street person next to you in the pew. It can be just as hard to find him in the unwelcoming host.

What makes us so afraid of the *other*? There's something in our ancient genetic memory that ratchets up our state of arousal when we meet a stranger—it's a survival mechanism that has kept our species alive for millennia by being wary of the unknown. But there's also a piece of our makeup that we talk about in more theological terms—the part that leaps to judgment about *that* person's sins. It's connected to knowing our own sinfulness and our tendency toward competition: *Well, she must be a worse sinner than I am—thank God!*

That woman who wanders into Simon's house when Jesus is dining there comes with her hair scandalously uncovered (Luke 7: 36–50). The dinner guests assume that she's a woman of the street, and in their view, she confirms it by acting in profoundly embarrassing ways, crying all over Jesus' feet and drying them with her hair and covering him with perfume. Jesus' host—and the rest of the dinner guests—were horrified that this was taking place in a "proper" house—they were more than a little worried about the gossip it would cause and appalled at the sort of person Jesus must be to let this woman do such things to him.

The scorn that some are willing to heap on those who are judged to have loved excessively or inappropriately is still pretty common. Yet it is this woman's loving response to Jesus that brings her pardon, and leads to Jesus' celebration of her right relationship with God. She doesn't even have to ask. Jesus seems to say that evidence of her pardon has already been given—full measure, pressed down, and overflowing—just like her tears and hair and cask of perfume.

It's the same message Jesus offers over and over: "Perfect love casts out fear" (1 John 4:18). It's actually our fear of the wretchedness within our own souls that pushes us away from our sisters and brothers. Fear is the only thing that keeps us from knowing God's love—and we most often discover it in the people around us. Jesus wasn't afraid to eat with sinners—Simon and the other dinner guests were sinners, too—and he wasn't afraid of what the woman of the city would do to his reputation.

The forgiven woman of the city is sister to the prodigal son who begs his father's forgiveness. They are both our siblings, and their experience is ours, too. Like them, we can rejoin the family if we're willing to let go of the fearful veneer of righteousness that covers our yearning to be fully known, because we don't quite think we're lovable. That veneer is the only thing between us and a whole-hearted "welcome home." It's risky to let that veneer be peeled away, but all we risk is love.

That's what Paul is talking about in his letter to the Galatians. He knows that all his work at observing the fine points of the law is like piling up the layers in a piece of plywood. Those layers of veneer may make plywood strong, but in human beings they have to be peeled away, or maybe traded for transparent ones. The layers won't right our relationship with God. Love will. Paul says, "If I build up again the very things that I once tore down, then I demonstrate that I am a sinner" (Galatians 2:18; my translation). The veneered self simply can't be vulnerable enough to receive the love that's being offered. Can we see the human heart yearning for love in *that* person over there? Can we recall our own yearning, and find the connection? That's what compassion is—opening ourselves to love.

Practicing compassion rather than judgment is one way the layers start to fly off. Think about all those dinner guests. The party's going to be far more interesting if we can find something to love about the curmudgeonly host and his buddies. Rejecting them is going to shut down any real possibility of compassion. It's risky, yes, but the only thing we risk is our own hearts, and the possibility they'll overflow as readily as that woman's tears. It's a big risk to let the layers go, but the only thing we risk is discovering a brother or sister under the skin.

Jesus invites us all to his moveable feast. He leaves that dinner party with Simon and goes off to visit other places in need of prodigal love and prodigious forgiveness. His companions, literally his tablemates, are the twelve apostles and "some women who had been cured of evil spirits and infirmities"—strong, healthy women, three of them, named Mary Magdalene, Joanna, and Susanna. Together with many others they supported and fed the community—they became hosts of the banquet.

Those who know the deep acceptance and love that come with healing and forgiveness can lose the defensive veneer that wants to shut out other sinners. They discover that covering their hair or hiding their tears or hoarding their rich perfume isn't the way that the beloved act, even if it makes others nervous. Eventually, it may even cure the anxious of their own fear by drawing them toward a seat at that heavenly banquet. There's room for us all at this table; there are tears of welcome and a kiss for the wanderer, and the sweet smell of home.

Want to join the feast? We are all welcome. Love has saved us, so enter in peace.

For Reflection

When have you been blessed by a surprising stranger?

Healing Division

As soon as they left the synagogue, they entered the house of Simon and Andrew, with James and John. Now Simon's mother-in-law was in bed with a fever, and they told him about her at once. He came and took her by the hand and lifted her up. Then the fever left her, and she began to serve them.

—MARK 1:29–31

A couple of years ago, I went to Egypt for a meeting of the primates of the Anglican Communion—the archbishops and presiding bishops of the thirty-eight national and international churches that make up the Anglican Communion.

One of the most intriguing conversations I had at the primates' meeting happened in a Bible study. An archbishop who has also served as a physician observed that he'd never met a blind person who didn't want to see. I countered by saying that blind people often develop ways of seeing that the sighted can never hope to match. He was insistent, however, that even those born blind always want to see. I know that's not universally true in the deaf culture. There is a strong—though not universal—sentiment in the deaf community that insists that deafness is a gift, not something to be cured.

It occurred to me that what God does in becoming human in Jesus is like choosing deafness or blindness—a limitation that allows other gifts to emerge. Jesus quite literally had insight into the human condition that could be shared in no other way.

What insights have your own limitations brought you? What have you seen and learned and felt and experienced through the challenges and traumas of your own life? What have pain, anger, and betrayal given you? There is gift and blessing in the midst of woundedness, and it's a part of our lives in Jesus, and part of our own resurrection.

That's what's going on with Simon's mother-in-law. Jesus has just come from healing a man in the synagogue to Simon and Andrew's house, where he discovers that Simon's mother-in-law is laid up with a fever. He takes her by the hand, raises her up, and the fever leaves, just as the spirit left the man in the synagogue. It seems that the people around the man in the synagogue looked for healing for their friend, and Simon and Andrew and the others in their house were looking for the same for the feverish woman. Sometimes we need our friends and family to look out for us.

Jesus raises her up—the Greek word in the gospel is the same one used to describe Jesus' resurrection. Peter's mother-in-law is quite literally raised up into new life. Blessed with this new life, her response is to serve—without further ado, she begins to wait on her family and her guests. She becomes the first deacon—the gospel writer uses the same word that's used by the people of the early church and the church today for those whose work is to go out from beyond the walls of the church into the community to care for the sick, the poor, and the marginalized. Her experience of illness— and the new life she receives—leads her to respond in service. That's the center of the ministry of deacons, and it's the center of all our lives as Christians, too.

I heard another very interesting story at that meeting in Egypt, about an immigrant in Canada who found sanctuary in a church. Sonia wasn't a legal immigrant, but the local Anglican church took her in while she struggled to get her request for asylum granted. The parishioners made a room for her in the basement, and looked after her for months. People flocked to her, crowding around, just to be in her presence—she became the local holy woman in that place. It made me think of Dame Julian, who lived in a little room connected to the church in Norwich, England, in the Middle Ages. She took on the ascetical way of living as an anchorite, mostly closed off from the world and a normal life in order to focus on her interior life. But the world wouldn't leave her alone. They kept coming to learn from her spiritual insight.

Is that experience of Sonia's or of Julian's an illness that should be cured? In the world's eyes, it's likely to be seen as a disability not to be able to go where and when you please, but it also has blessings. Both of them seem to have been holy women—and the word *holy* is another variation on the same root that gives us the words *whole* and *healthy*.

There are many kinds of healing, and they don't all come with surgery or drugs. We're finally beginning to do some good theology around the different conditions in which human beings find themselves, particularly around what we call physical and mental handicaps. Some have pointed out that all of us are disabled at some point in our lives—we start out that way as babies and pretty much end up that way when we've grown old—and that at the most we can say that we are temporarily able-bodied. Yet we have a tendency to say that this state is normal, and that another condition is a disability that needs to be fixed. It tends to be a pretty one-sided kind of definition, rather than listening to the person concerned about what he or she thinks.

There are people who appear to be profoundly disabled in the world's terms who nevertheless live lives that look healed. What about Stephen Hawking? He's lived for more than forty years with amyotrophic lateral sclerosis—Lou Gehrig's disease—a condition that affects the nerve cells in the brain and spinal cord that control voluntary muscle movement. His mind, though, has blessed the world with profound contributions to physics and mathematics. I'm not implying that he wouldn't choose to live in another way if he could, but that while some call him handicapped, he could just as well call most of us more ordinary mortals intellectually handicapped. Definitions are not as simple as they might seem.

But for Jesus, disability always means isolation, and his healing is always a restoration to community. The man who's been healed in the synagogue can't take part in the usual religious life because he has an "unclean" spirit. Simon's mother-in-law is isolated because of her fever. When you look at the healing stories in the gospels, you quickly see that Jesus may heal the physical illness or the psychological demon, but that kind of healing is almost always followed up with a demonstration that a person becomes whole only in relation to the larger community. Jesus tells the onlookers to feed Simon's mother-in-law (Mark 5:43), or he sends the lepers to visit the priest so they can get their ticket back into community life (Luke 17:11–19). That is the goal of healing—a fuller and more abundant life. Simon's mother-in-law understands that as she responds to her healing with an act of community building.

The divisions today in The Episcopal Church and other denominations over the equality—or lack of equality—of people who are gay or lesbian have happened because some think that gay people are sick. Many in the church have energetically resisted that definition, and they are being raised up to more abundant life as they claim the blessing of God's love for all. If the church's healing is to continue, all of us will need to give evidence of it by working to build a more obviously healed community around us. That includes the kind of diaconal ministry that Simon's mother-in-law models—the ministry that's involved in feeding the hungry and sheltering the homeless.

When people and parishes have left The Episcopal Church because gay people have been welcomed into the congregation and ordained, it's often resulted in a lot of pain for those who remain. They will be healed as they give evidence of their own healing. Their resurrection has something to do with how they find the blessings in that pain and separation and sense of betrayal. Responding with vengeance only causes more wounds. Instead, healing lies in remembering the pain in their own hearts rather than adding to the pain in someone else's. Wholeness comes of counting wounds as a blessing, and offering generosity in abundance.

Being vilified by fellow believers is not an invitation to roll over and play dead, or to respond defensively to the charge others have made of being unchristian, or morally depraved, or spiritually handicapped. That is only the definition of others, and it won't be fixed by telling them that they're the ones who are sick.

God calls each and every one of us beloved. Those who long for the inclusion of gay brothers and lesbian sisters have been blessed by God with a wider vision for what a healed and beloved community might look like. We're supposed to give evidence of that healing, in the sense that the Apostle Paul is talking about: Proclaim the gospel because you have no choice (1 Corinthians 9:16–18).

Our healing is caught up in that obligation. It is a prescription for the well-being of the world. We must speak good news to all who will listen, and we will continue to be raised into new life. Good news, not vengeance, will heal our neighbors. Our prescription for new life is to take those two tablets—the ones Moses got, inscribed with the commandments—and call on God if the pain returns. Doctor's orders!

For Reflection

Think about the unfortunate divisions in your own life and your own family. What has your path to healing been?

Finding God in Dissent

At that very hour some Pharisees came and said to him, "Get away from here, for Herod wants to kill you." He said to them, "Go and tell that fox for me, 'Listen, I am casting out demons and performing cures today and tomorrow, and on the third day I finish my work. Yet today, tomorrow, and the next day I must be on my way, because it is impossible for a prophet to be killed outside of Jerusalem.'"

—LUKE 13:31–33

I recently visited a church in Kentucky, where I heard something about the joys and challenges of life in rural and small communities. One man told of the Sunday he was scheduled to take a visiting priest to dinner after the service. He got a phone call during church, though, telling him that his bull had escaped from the pasture—and not for the first time. He was torn between competing duties—would he take the bull home or the priest?

Another man said he'd also had to deal with escaping bulls and horses, and recounted the well-remembered occasion when the flock of chickens next door to the church was destroyed by a bunch of weasels.

I don't get to spend nearly enough time in the country. My encounters with wildlife and livestock are limited to what I see when I'm out running early in the morning—and in New York City, I'm lucky to see a pigeon or a seagull.

The gospels are filled with stories about Jesus and his encounters with other creatures in his environment. He uses images of the countryside freely—he talks about sheep and shepherds, wolves and sheep-stealers, as well as vineyards, harvests, and fishing expeditions. He rides a donkey. And in the gospel of Luke, he calls Herod a fox.

Farmers and herders know about foxes, but they're not much of a threat to sheep or cattle or horses. They are only a threat to small livestock such as poultry and rabbits. And that's where Jesus goes with his image: "Go tell that fox Herod that I'm busy, and I'll see him later. I will turn up in Jerusalem when it's time." It's a not-so-subtle way of putting King Herod in his place. Jesus has a pretty clear sense of what's waiting for him in Jerusalem, but he goes on his own terms—when he's good and ready—not because some fox is chasing him. We think of foxes as clever, but Jesus is actually offering an insult. Foxes are small-time predators, and it's a fitting image for Herod, who has to answer to Rome and definitely doesn't sit at the top of the food chain. Herod, the Roman-appointed "king of the Jews," is really just a petty harasser of the small and weak.

Jesus keeps pushing the image of the fox. "Jerusalem, Jerusalem," he laments as his disciples listen, "how I've tried to gather you up, like a hen gathering her chicks under her wings. But you weren't interested" (Luke 31:34; my translation). There's a fox in the henhouse, and Jesus as mother hen wants to gather up those vulnerable chicks and protect them. That image of God as a brooding hen is an ancient one—maybe most familiar in the verse in Compline, the ancient service of Christian evening prayer: "Keep us, O Lord, as the apple of your eye; hide us under the shadow of your wings" (Psalm 17:8), and it appears in several other psalms as well. Sheltering the chicks is one more example of God's care for the least and most vulnerable among us.

It's not a pretty thing when a fox gets in the henhouse. Congregations wracked by the misbehavior of leaders know something about that, and in The Episcopal Church in the past few years there's been a fair amount of that. A fox sashays into the henhouse—a petty tyrant claims the divine right of judgment, power over life and death—and wreaks havoc with God's creatures. It happens around us all the time, when some human tyrant resolves to control other people's lives and decide who's in and who's out of the community. Maybe the local bishop decides that he'll only permit priests to move into the diocese who agree with him on every important issue, no matter what their other gifts or shortcomings might be. Maybe a leader tries to expel other leaders who disagree on some issue, but are there to provide a balance in the system. The fox in the henhouse is at the root of all kinds of slavery and oppression and exploitation—from the bully in the schoolyard to leaders of nations who believe their government is a private bank account. Nothing keeps those tyrants in control except the fear of those beneath them.

In Liberia several years ago, the warlords were forced to the negotiating table by people who finally said, "No more—we've had enough." A large group of market women, sick and tired of being unable to feed their children and watching their loved ones die and disappear, finally got organized and said *no*. We're going to accompany you to the table, they insisted, and sit outside this meeting place, and we're going to stay here until you figure out how the people of this nation can live together in peace.

The Taliban, too, stay in power through intimidation. They shut down girls' schools and insist that women can't go out and lead ordinary lives in public. They bribe officials and shoot anybody who resists their authority. The violence in the Holy Land is rooted in similar kinds of fear-mongering on all sides. The rabid partisanship in our own Congress recently has a lot of fear wrapped up in it, as one faction or another insists that citizens will be gored by health-care reform or that jobs or national security will be jeopardized by changes in immigration policies. Terrorists and tyrants derive their power from the fear they engender in others.

Jesus challenges the people of Jerusalem—and us—to take shelter in a place that isn't based in violence. When his listeners decline the challenge, he says, "Well, it's your house—keep it—you just try and live in it." He's not abandoning them, but they're not going to notice him until they recognize that he comes from the owner of the henhouse. He comes from the God who dwells in Jerusalem's big house, the Temple. It's not Rome's henhouse—it belongs to the mother bird, and that Roman fox is not going to protect them.

The henhouse has room for all sorts of creatures if they're looking for a home. A skunk can find shelter there if it wants to, and a bull, and even a fox—if it'll give up devouring chicks.

God has always promised to gather us up under God's wings and protect us from foxes. And God's promises usually come in pretty surprising ways. In a deep and terrifying darkness, God promises Abraham as many descendants as the stars in the sky and a land for his people brimming with milk and honey (Genesis 22:17). And in the midst of that terrifying darkness and those amazing, disturbing promises, God also gives Abraham the gift of sleep and dreaming, where he shelters under the wings of a trustworthy God.

Congregations troubled by authoritarian, abusive, or self-interested leadership won't heal until they let go of fear and terror and remember the trust and the love of God for all, even those who have injured them. Remember who came to warn Jesus about Herod. It was the Pharisees, the people Christians too often love to hate. It's a reminder that even our supposed enemies can be a gift. Our healing requires us to put away fear of those who have caused us hurt.

Consider the story of Christ Church in Lexington, Kentucky, where a couple of years ago parishioners celebrated a remarkable piece of healing. Members of First African Baptist Church joined members of Christ Church in letting go of some of the old hurt of slavery as they remembered and celebrated the life of the Reverend London Ferrell and his ministry among slaves, free blacks, and even slaveholders in Lexington. He is the only African American buried in the old Episcopal Burying Grounds. Even in 1854, years before the Emancipation Proclamation, his burial there signaled the deep knowledge that we can and do shelter under the same wings of that ancient mother hen, the God who is making all things new.

Fear has no place in the henhouse, and it won't build the reign of God. *"Fear is useless,"* declares Jesus; "what is needed is trust" (Luke 8:50; my translation). We can only address the injustices in our parishes and our communities and our denominations, and welcome into the henhouse other chicks who need shelter, when we trust in God, cast out fear, and name the fox for the petty tyrant he is.

For Reflection

Where have you encountered foxes in your own life and your own community? How have you responded?

Notes

Introduction

1. Rachel Groman, "The Cost of Lack of Health Insurance" (paper, American College of Physicians, May 7, 2004), www.acponline.org/advocacy/where_we_stand/access/cost.pdf.

Serving the Poor

1. *Human Reproduction,* vol. 20, no. 9 (August 23, 2005): 2483–88.
2. Economic Policy Institute website, www.epi.org/content/budget_calculator/?family_type=1P1C&state=DC&area_name=Washington-Arlington-Alexandria%2C+DC-VA-MD+HUD+Metro+FMR+Area.
3. District of Columbia Department of Employment Services website, http://newsroom.dc.gov/show.aspx/agency/does/section/2/release/20222.

Creative Survival

1. Julia Dinsmore, *My Name Is Child of God ... Not "Those People": A First Person Look at Poverty* (Minneapolis: Augsburg Fortress, 2007).
2. Edward Ball, *Slaves in the Family* (New York: Ballantine Books, 1998).

Provoking Love

1. Eugene H. Peterson, *The Message: The Bible in Contemporary Language* (Colorado Springs, Co.: NavPress, 1993).

The Ecology of Faith

1. Sarah Coakley, "Evolution and Sacrifice," *Christian Century,* October 20, 2009, www.christiancentury.org/article.lasso?id=7872.

Who Is Jesus in the World Today?

1. *The Book of Common Prayer* (New York: Oxford University Press, 1979), 372.

Living the Questions

1. *The Book of Common Prayer*, 220.

Fossils

1. Interview, *U.S. News & World Report*, July 26, 1989.

Suggestions for Further Reading

Alkire, Sabina. *What Can One Person Do? Faith to Heal a Broken World*. New York: Church Publishing, 2005.

Kidder, Tracy. *Mountains beyond Mountains: The Quest of Dr. Paul Farmer, a Man Who Would Cure the World*. New York: Random House, 2009.

Kristof, Nicholas D. and Sheryl WuDunn. *Half the Sky: Turning Oppression into Opportunity for Women Worldwide*. New York: Vintage, 2010.

Mortenson, Greg, and David Oliver Relin. *Three Cups of Tea: One Man's Mission to Promote Peace One School at a Time*. New York: Penguin, 2007.

Pollan, Michael. *Food Rules: An Eater's Manual*. New York: Penguin, 2009.

Schwab, A. Wayne. *When the Members Are the Missionaries: An Extraordinary Calling for Ordinary People*. Plattsburgh, NY: Member Mission Press, 2002.

Stearns, Richard. *The Hole in Our Gospel: What Does God Expect of Us?* Nashville: Thomas Nelson, 2010.

Children's Spirituality

Adam & Eve's First Sunset: God's New Day
by Sandy Eisenberg Sasso; Full-color illus. by Joani Keller Rothenberg 9 x 12, 32 pp, Full-color illus., HC,
978-1-58023-177-0 **$17.95*** *For ages 4 & up*

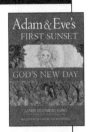

Because Nothing Looks Like God
by Lawrence Kushner and Karen Kushner; Full-color illus. by Dawn W. Majewski
Invites parents and children to explore the questions we all have about God.
11 x 8½, 32 pp, Full-color illus., HC, 978-1-58023-092-6 **$17.99*** *For ages 4 & up*

Also available: **Teacher's Guide** 8½ x 11, 22 pp, PB, 978-1-58023-140-4 **$6.95** *For ages 5–8*

But God Remembered: Stories of Women from Creation to the
Promised Land   *by Sandy Eisenberg Sasso; Full-color illus. by Bethanne Andersen*
A fascinating collection of four different stories of women only briefly mentioned in biblical tradition and religious texts.
9 x 12, 32 pp, Full-color illus., Quality PB, 978-1-58023-372-9 **$8.99*** *For ages 8 & up*

Cain & Abel: Finding the Fruits of Peace
by Sandy Eisenberg Sasso; Full-color illus. by Joani Keller Rothenberg
A sensitive recasting of the ancient tale shows we have the power to deal with anger in positive ways. "Editor's Choice." —American Library Association's *Booklist*
9 x 12, 32 pp, Full-color illus., HC, 978-1-58023-123-7 **$16.95*** *For ages 5 & up*

Does God Hear My Prayer?
by August Gold; Full-color photos by Diane Hardy Waller
Introduces preschoolers and young readers to prayer and how it helps them express their own emotions.
10 x 8½, 32 pp, Full-color photo illus., Quality PB, 978-1-59473-102-0 **$8.99** *For ages 3–6*

The 11th Commandment: Wisdom from Our Children *by The Children of America*
"If there were an Eleventh Commandment, what would it be?" Children of many religious denominations across America answer this question—in their own drawings and words. "A rare book of spiritual celebration for all people, of all ages, for all time." —*Bookviews*   8 x 10, 48 pp, Full-color illus., HC, 978-1-879045-46-0 **$16.95***
For all ages

For Heaven's Sake *by Sandy Eisenberg Sasso; Full-color illus. by Kathryn Kunz Finney*
Heaven is often found where you least expect it.
9 x 12, 32 pp, Full-color illus., HC, 978-1-58023-054-4 **$16.95*** *For ages 4 & up*

God in Between *by Sandy Eisenberg Sasso; Full-color illus. by Sally Sweetland*
A magical, mythical tale that teaches that God can be found where we are.
9 x 12, 32 pp, Full-color illus., HC, 978-1-879045-86-6 **$16.95*** *For ages 4 & up*

God's Paintbrush: Special 10th Anniversary Edition
Invites children of all faiths and backgrounds to encounter God through moments in their own lives. 11 x 8½, 32 pp, Full-color illus., HC, 978-1-58023-195-4 **$17.95*** *For ages 4 & up*

Also available: **God's Paintbrush Teacher's Guide**
8½ x 11, 32 pp, PB, 978-1-879045-57-6 **$8.95**

God's Paintbrush Celebration Kit: A Spiritual Activity Kit for Teachers and
Students of All Faiths, All Backgrounds 9½ x 12, 40 Full-color Activity Sheets & Teacher Folder w/ complete instructions, HC, 978-1-58023-050-6 **$21.95**
Additional activity sheets available:
8-Student Activity Sheet Pack (40 sheets/5 sessions), 978-1-58023-058-2 **$19.95**
Single-Student Activity Sheet Pack (5 sessions), 978-1-58023-059-9 **$3.95**

I Am God's Paintbrush (A Board Book)
by Sandy Eisenberg Sasso; Full-color illus. by Annette Compton
5 x 5, 24 pp, Full-color illus., Board Book, 978-1-59473-265-2 **$7.99** *For ages 0–4*

* A book from Jewish Lights, SkyLight Paths' sister imprint

Judaism / Christianity / Islam / Interfaith

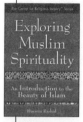

Exploring Muslim Spirituality: An Introduction to the Beauty of Islam
by Hussein Rashid Moves beyond basic information to explore what Islam means to a believer—written by a believer. 6 x 9, 192 pp (est), Quality PB, 978-1-59473-277-5 **$16.99**

Getting to the Heart of Interfaith
The Eye-Opening, Hope-Filled Friendship of a Pastor, a Rabbi and a Sheikh
by Pastor Don Mackenzie, Rabbi Ted Falcon and Sheikh Jamal Rahman
Offers many insights and encouragements for individuals and groups who want to tap into the promise of interfaith dialogue. 6 x 9, 192 pp, Quality PB, 978-1-59473-263-8 **$16.99**

Hearing the Call across Traditions: Readings on Faith and Service
Edited by Adam Davis; Foreword by Eboo Patel Explores the connections between faith, service and social justice through the prose, verse and sacred texts of the world's great faith traditions. 6 x 9, 352 pp, HC, 978-1-59473-264-5 **$29.99**

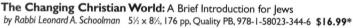

How to Do Good & Avoid Evil: A Global Ethic from the Sources of Judaism *by Hans Küng and Rabbi Walter Homolka; Translated by Rev. Dr. John Bowden* Explores how Judaism's ethical principles can help all religions work together toward a more peaceful humankind. 6 x 9, 224 pp, HC, 978-1-59473-255-3 **$19.99**

Blessed Relief: What Christians Can Learn from Buddhists about Suffering
by Gordon Peerman 6 x 9, 208 pp, Quality PB, 978-1-59473-252-2 **$16.99**

The Changing Christian World: A Brief Introduction for Jews
by Rabbi Leonard A. Schoolman 5½ x 8½, 176 pp, Quality PB, 978-1-58023-344-6 **$16.99***

Christians & Jews in Dialogue: Learning in the Presence of the Other *by Mary C. Boys and Sara S. Lee; Foreword by Dorothy C. Bass* 6 x 9, 240 pp, Quality PB, 978-1-59473-254-6 **$18.99**; HC, 978-1-59473-144-0 **$21.99**

Disaster Spiritual Care: Practical Clergy Responses to Community, Regional and National Tragedy *Edited by Rabbi Stephen B. Roberts, BCJC, and Rev. Willard W.C. Ashley, Sr., DMin, DH*
6 x 9, 384 pp, HC, 978-1-59473-240-9 **$40.00**

InterActive Faith: The Essential Interreligious Community-Building Handbook
Edited by Rev. Bud Heckman with Rori Picker Neiss; Foreword by Rev. Dirk Ficca
6 x 9, 304 pp, HC, 978-1-59473-237-9 **$29.99**

The Jewish Approach to God: A Brief Introduction for Christians
by Rabbi Neil Gillman, PhD 5½ x 8½, 192 pp, Quality PB, 978-1-58023-190-9 **$16.95***

The Jewish Approach to Repairing the World (*Tikkun Olam*): A Brief Introduction for Christians *by Rabbi Elliot N. Dorff, PhD, with Rev. Cory Willson*
5½ x 8½, 256 pp, Quality PB, 978-1-58023-349-1 **$16.99***

The Jewish Connection to Israel, the Promised Land: A Brief Introduction for Christians *by Rabbi Eugene Korn, PhD* 5½ x 8½, 192 pp, Quality PB, 978-1-58023-318-7 **$14.99***

Jewish Holidays: A Brief Introduction for Christians *by Rabbi Kerry M. Olitzky and Rabbi Daniel Judson* 5½ x 8½, 176 pp, Quality PB, 978-1-58023-302-6 **$16.99***

Jewish Ritual: A Brief Introduction for Christians
by Rabbi Kerry M. Olitzky and Rabbi Daniel Judson 5½ x 8½, 144 pp, Quality PB, 978-1-58023-210-4 **$14.99***

Jewish Spirituality: A Brief Introduction for Christians *by Rabbi Lawrence Kushner* 5½ x 8½, 112 pp, Quality PB, 978-1-58023-150-3 **$12.95***

A Jewish Understanding of the New Testament *by Rabbi Samuel Sandmel;*
New preface by Rabbi David Sandmel 5½ x 8½, 368 pp, Quality PB, 978-1-59473-048-1 **$19.99***

Modern Jews Engage the New Testament: Enhancing Jewish Well-Being in a Christian Environment *by Rabbi Michael J. Cook, PhD* 6 x 9, 416 pp, HC 978-1-58023-313-2 **$29.99***

Talking about God: Exploring the Meaning of Religious Life with Kierkegaard, Buber, Tillich and Heschel *by Daniel F. Polish, PhD* 6 x 9, 160 pp, Quality PB, 978-1-59473-272-0 **$16.99**

We Jews and Jesus: Exploring Theological Differences for Mutual Understanding
by Rabbi Samuel Sandmel; New preface by Rabbi David Sandmel
6 x 9, 192 pp, Quality PB, 978-1-59473-208-9 **$16.99**

Who Are the *Real* Chosen People? The Meaning of Chosenness in Judaism, Christianity and Islam *by Reuven Firestone, PhD*
6 x 9, 176 pp, Quality PB, 978-1-59473-290-4 **$16.99**

* A book from Jewish Lights, SkyLight Paths' sister imprint

Bible Stories / Folktales

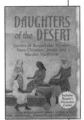

Abraham's Bind & Other Bible Tales of Trickery, Folly, Mercy and Love by Michael J. Caduto
New retellings of episodes in the lives of familiar biblical characters explore relevant life lessons. 6 x 9, 224 pp, HC, 978-1-59473-186-0 **$19.99**

Daughters of the Desert: Stories of Remarkable Women from Christian, Jewish and Muslim Traditions by Claire Rudolf Murphy, Meghan Nuttall Sayres, Mary Cronk Farrell, Sarah Conover and Betsy Wharton
Breathes new life into the old tales of our female ancestors in faith. Uses traditional scriptural passages as starting points, then with vivid detail fills in historical context and place. Chapters reveal the voices of Sarah, Hagar, Huldah, Esther, Salome, Mary Magdalene, Lydia, Khadija, Fatima and many more. Historical fiction ideal for readers of all ages.
5½ x 8½, 192 pp, Quality PB, 978-1-59473-106-8 **$14.99** Inc. reader's discussion guide
HC, 978-1-893361-72-0 **$19.95**

The Triumph of Eve & Other Subversive Bible Tales
by Matt Biers-Ariel
These engaging retellings of familiar Bible stories are witty, often hilarious and always profound. They invite you to grapple with questions and issues that are often hidden in the original texts.
5½ x 8½, 192 pp, Quality PB, 978-1-59473-176-1 **$14.99**

Also available: **The Triumph of Eve Teacher's Guide**
8½ x 11, 44 pp, PB, 978-1-59473-152-5 **$8.99**

Wisdom in the Telling
Finding Inspiration and Grace in Traditional Folktales and Myths Retold
by Lorraine Hartin-Gelardi
6 x 9, 192 pp, HC, 978-1-59473-185-3 **$19.99**

Religious Etiquette / Reference

How to Be a Perfect Stranger, 4th Edition: The Essential Religious Etiquette Handbook Edited by Stuart M. Matlins and Arthur J. Magida
The indispensable guidebook to help the well-meaning guest when visiting other people's religious ceremonies. A straightforward guide to the rituals and celebrations of the major religions and denominations in the United States and Canada from the perspective of an interested guest of any other faith, based on information obtained from authorities of each religion. Belongs in every living room, library and office. Covers:
African American Methodist Churches • Assemblies of God • Bahá'í • Baptist • Buddhist • Christian Church (Disciples of Christ) • Christian Science (Church of Christ, Scientist) • Churches of Christ • Episcopalian and Anglican • Hindu • Islam • Jehovah's Witnesses • Jewish • Lutheran • Mennonite/Amish • Methodist • Mormon (Church of Jesus Christ of Latter-day Saints) • Native American/First Nations • Orthodox Churches • Pentecostal Church of God • Presbyterian • Quaker (Religious Society of Friends) • Reformed Church in America/Canada • Roman Catholic • Seventh-day Adventist • Sikh • Unitarian Universalist • United Church of Canada • United Church of Christ

"The things Miss Manners forgot to tell us about religion."
— *Los Angeles Times*

"Finally, for those inclined to undertake their own spiritual journeys ... tells visitors what to expect." — *New York Times*
6 x 9, 432 pp, Quality PB, 978-1-59473-140-2 **$19.99**

The Perfect Stranger's Guide to Funerals and Grieving Practices: A Guide to Etiquette in Other People's Religious Ceremonies Edited by Stuart M. Matlins
6 x 9, 240 pp, Quality PB, 978-1-893361-20-1 **$16.95**

The Perfect Stranger's Guide to Wedding Ceremonies: A Guide to Etiquette in Other People's Religious Ceremonies Edited by Stuart M. Matlins
6 x 9, 208 pp, Quality PB, 978-1-893361-19-5 **$16.95**

Spirituality of the Seasons

Autumn: A Spiritual Biography of the Season
Edited by Gary Schmidt and Susan M. Felch; Illus. by Mary Azarian
Rejoice in autumn as a time of preparation and reflection. Includes Wendell Berry, David James Duncan, Robert Frost, A. Bartlett Giamatti, E. B. White, P. D. James, Julian of Norwich, Garret Keizer, Tracy Kidder, Anne Lamott, May Sarton.
6 x 9, 320 pp, b/w illus., Quality PB, 978-1-59473-118-1 **$18.99**

Spring: A Spiritual Biography of the Season
Edited by Gary Schmidt and Susan M. Felch; Illus. by Mary Azarian
Explore the gentle unfurling of spring and reflect on how nature celebrates rebirth and renewal. Includes Jane Kenyon, Lucy Larcom, Harry Thurston, Nathaniel Hawthorne, Noel Perrin, Annie Dillard, Martha Ballard, Barbara Kingsolver, Dorothy Wordsworth, Donald Hall, David Brill, Lionel Basney, Isak Dinesen, Paul Laurence Dunbar. 6 x 9, 352 pp, b/w illus., Quality PB, 978-1-59473-246-1 **$18.99**

Summer: A Spiritual Biography of the Season
Edited by Gary Schmidt and Susan M. Felch; Illus. by Barry Moser
"A sumptuous banquet.... These selections lift up an exquisite wholeness found within an everyday sophistication." — ★ *Publishers Weekly* starred review
Includes Anne Lamott, Luci Shaw, Ray Bradbury, Richard Selzer, Thomas Lynch, Walt Whitman, Carl Sandburg, Sherman Alexie, Madeleine L'Engle, Jamaica Kincaid.
6 x 9, 304 pp, b/w illus., Quality PB, 978-1-59473-183-9 **$18.99**
HC, 978-1-59473-083-2 **$21.99**

Winter: A Spiritual Biography of the Season
Edited by Gary Schmidt and Susan M. Felch; Illus. by Barry Moser
"This outstanding anthology features top-flight nature and spirituality writers on the fierce, inexorable season of winter.... Remarkably lively and warm, despite the icy subject." — ★ *Publishers Weekly* starred review
Includes Will Campbell, Rachel Carson, Annie Dillard, Donald Hall, Ron Hansen, Jane Kenyon, Jamaica Kincaid, Barry Lopez, Kathleen Norris, John Updike, E. B. White.
6 x 9, 288 pp, b/w illus., Deluxe PB w/ flaps, 978-1-893361-92-8 **$18.95**;
HC, 978-1-893361-53-9 **$21.95**

Spirituality / Animal Companions

Blessing the Animals: Prayers and Ceremonies to Celebrate God's Creatures, Wild and Tame *Edited and with Introductions by Lynn L. Caruso*
5¼ x 7¼, 256 pp, Quality PB, 978-1-59473-253-9 **$15.99**; HC, 978-1-59473-145-7 **$19.99**

Remembering My Pet: A Kid's Own Spiritual Workbook for When a Pet Dies
by Nechama Liss-Levinson, PhD, and Rev. Molly Phinney Baskette, MDiv; Foreword by Lynn L. Caruso
8 x 10, 48 pp, 2-color text, HC, 978-1-59473-221-8 **$16.99**

What Animals Can Teach Us about Spirituality: Inspiring Lessons from Wild and Tame Creatures *by Diana L. Guerrero* 6 x 9, 176 pp, Quality PB, 978-1-893361-84-3 **$16.95**

Spirituality—A Week Inside

Lighting the Lamp of Wisdom: A Week Inside a Yoga Ashram
by John Ittner; Foreword by Dr. David Frawley
6 x 9, 192 pp, b/w photos, Quality PB, 978-1-893361-52-2 **$15.95**

Making a Heart for God: A Week Inside a Catholic Monastery
by Dianne Aprile; Foreword by Brother Patrick Hart, ocso
6 x 9, 224 pp, b/w photos, Quality PB, 978-1-893361-49-2 **$16.95**

Waking Up: A Week Inside a Zen Monastery
by Jack Maguire; Foreword by John Daido Loori, Roshi
6 x 9, 224 pp, b/w photos, Quality PB, 978-1-893361-55-3 **$16.95**; HC, 978-1-893361-13-3 **$21.95**

Spirituality & Crafts

Beading—The Creative Spirit: Finding Your Sacred Center through the Art of Beadwork *by Rev. Wendy Ellsworth*
Invites you on a spiritual pilgrimage into the kaleidoscope world of glass and color.   7 x 9, 240 pp, 8-page color insert, 40+ b/w photos and 40 diagrams, Quality PB, 978-1-59473-267-6 **$18.99**

Contemplative Crochet: A Hands-On Guide for Interlocking Faith and Craft *by Cindy Crandall-Frazier; Foreword by Linda Skolnik*
Illuminates the spiritual lessons you can learn through crocheting.
7 x 9, 208 pp, b/w photos, Quality PB, 978-1-59473-238-6 **$16.99**

The Knitting Way: A Guide to Spiritual Self-Discovery
by Linda Skolnik and Janice MacDaniels Examines how you can explore and strengthen your spiritual life through knitting.
7 x 9, 240 pp, b/w photos, Quality PB, 978-1-59473-079-5 **$16.99**

The Painting Path: Embodying Spiritual Discovery through Yoga, Brush and Color *by Linda Novick; Foreword by Richard Segalman*
Explores the divine connection you can experience through art.
7 x 9, 208 pp, 8-page color insert, plus b/w photos, Quality PB, 978-1-59473-226-3 **$18.99**

The Quilting Path: A Guide to Spiritual Discovery through Fabric, Thread and Kabbalah *by Louise Silk*
Explores how to cultivate personal growth through quilt making.
7 x 9, 192 pp, b/w photos and illus., Quality PB, 978-1-59473-206-5 **$16.99**

The Scrapbooking Journey: A Hands-On Guide to Spiritual Discovery
by Cory Richardson-Lauve; Foreword by Stacy Julian Reveals how this craft can become a practice used to deepen and shape your life.
7 x 9, 176 pp, 8-page color insert, plus b/w photos, Quality PB, 978-1-59473-216-4 **$18.99**

The Soulwork of Clay: A Hands-On Approach to Spirituality
by Marjory Zoet Bankson; Photos by Peter Bankson
Takes you through the seven-step process of making clay into a pot, drawing parallels at each stage to the process of spiritual growth.
7 x 9, 192 pp, b/w photos, Quality PB, 978-1-59473-249-2 **$16.99**

Kabbalah / Enneagram
(Books from Jewish Lights Publishing, SkyLight Paths' sister imprint)

Cast in God's Image: Discover Your Personality Type Using the Enneagram and Kabbalah
by Rabbi Howard A. Addison 7 x 9, 176 pp, Quality PB, 978-1-58023-124-4 **$16.95**

Ehyeh: A Kabbalah for Tomorrow *by Dr. Arthur Green*
6 x 9, 224 pp, Quality PB, 978-1-58023-213-5 **$16.99**

The Enneagram and Kabbalah, 2nd Edition: Reading Your Soul
by Rabbi Howard A. Addison 6 x 9, 192 pp, Quality PB, 978-1-58023-229-6 **$16.99**

The Gift of Kabbalah: Discovering the Secrets of Heaven, Renewing Your Life on Earth
by Tamar Frankiel, PhD 6 x 9, 256 pp, Quality PB, 978-1-58023-141-1 **$16.95**

God in Your Body: Kabbalah, Mindfulness and Embodied Spiritual Practice
by Jay Michaelson 6 x 9, 272 pp, Quality PB, 978-1-58023-304-0 **$18.99**

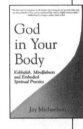

Kabbalah: A Brief Introduction for Christians
by Tamar Frankiel, PhD 5½ x 8½, 208 pp, Quality PB, 978-1-58023-303-3 **$16.99**

Zohar: Annotated & Explained *Translation & Annotation by Daniel C. Matt; Foreword by Andrew Harvey* 5½ x 8½, 176 pp, Quality PB, 978-1-893361-51-5 **$15.99**

Spirituality

Creative Aging: Rethinking Retirement and Non-Retirement in a Changing World *by Marjory Zoet Bankson*
Offers creative ways to nourish our calling and discover meaning and purpose in our older years. 6 x 9, 160 pp, Quality PB, 978-1-59473-281-2 **$16.99**

Laugh Your Way to Grace: Reclaiming the Spiritual Power of Humor
by Rev. Susan Sparks A powerful, humorous case for laughter as a spiritual, healing path. 6 x 9, 176 pp, Quality PB, 978-1-59473-280-5 **$16.99**

Living into Hope: A Call to Spiritual Action for Such a Time as This
by Rev. Dr. Joan Brown Campbell; Foreword by Karen Armstrong
A visionary minister speaks out on the pressing issues that face us today, offering inspiration and challenge. 6 x 9, 144 pp (est), HC, 978-1-59473-283-6 **$21.99**

Claiming Earth as Common Ground: The Ecological Crisis through the Lens of Faith *by Andrea Cohen-Kiener; Foreword by Rev. Sally Bingham*
Inspires us to work across denominational lines in order to fulfill our sacred imperative to care for God's creation. 6 x 9, 192 pp, Quality PB, 978-1-59473-261-4 **$16.99**

Bread, Body, Spirit: Finding the Sacred in Food
Edited and with Introductions by Alice Peck 6 x 9, 224 pp, Quality PB, 978-1-59473-242-3 **$19.99**

Creating a Spiritual Retirement: A Guide to the Unseen Possibilities in Our Lives
by Molly Srode 6 x 9, 208 pp, b/w photos, Quality PB, 978-1-59473-050-4 **$14.99**

Finding Hope: Cultivating God's Gift of a Hopeful Spirit
by Marcia Ford; Foreword by Andrea Jaeger 8 x 8, 176 pp, Quality PB, 978-1-59473-211-9 **$16.99**

Hearing the Call across Traditions: Readings on Faith and Service
Edited by Adam Davis; Foreword by Eboo Patel 6 x 9, 352 pp, HC, 978-1-59473-264-5 **$29.99**

Honoring Motherhood: Prayers, Ceremonies & Blessings
Edited and with Introductions by Lynn L. Caruso 5 x 7¼, 272 pp, HC, 978-1-59473-239-3 **$19.99**

Journeys of Simplicity: Traveling Light with Thomas Merton, Bashō, Edward Abbey, Annie Dillard & Others *by Philip Harnden*
5 x 7¼, 144 pp, Quality PB, 978-1-59473-181-5 **$12.99**; 128 pp, HC, 978-1-893361-76-8 **$16.95**

Keeping Spiritual Balance as We Grow Older: More than 65 Creative Ways to Use Purpose, Prayer, and the Power of Spirit to Build a Meaningful Retirement
by Molly and Bernie Srode 8 x 8, 224 pp, Quality PB, 978-1-59473-042-9 **$16.99**

The Losses of Our Lives: The Sacred Gifts of Renewal in Everyday Loss
by Dr. Nancy Copeland-Payton 6 x 9, 192 pp, HC, 978-1-59473-271-3 **$19.99**

Money and the Way of Wisdom: Insights from the Book of Proverbs
by Timothy J. Sandoval, PhD 6 x 9, 192 pp, Quality PB, 978-1-59473-245-4 **$16.99**

Next to Godliness: Finding the Sacred in Housekeeping
Edited by Alice Peck 6 x 9, 224 pp, Quality PB, 978-1-59473-214-0 **$19.99**

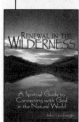

Renewal in the Wilderness: A Spiritual Guide to Connecting with God in the Natural World *by John Lionberger*
6 x 9, 176 pp, b/w photos, Quality PB, 978-1-59473-219-5 **$16.99**

Sacred Attention: A Spiritual Practice for Finding God in the Moment
by Margaret D. McGee 6 x 9, 144 pp, Quality PB, 978-1-59473-291-1 **$16.99**

Soul Fire: Accessing Your Creativity
by Thomas Ryan, CSP 6 x 9, 160 pp, Quality PB, 978-1-59473-243-0 **$16.99**

A Spirituality for Brokenness: Discovering Your Deepest Self in Difficult Times
by Terry Taylor 6 x 9, 176 pp, Quality PB, 978-1-59473-229-4 **$16.99**

Spiritually Incorrect: Finding God in All the *Wrong* Places *by Dan Wakefield; Illus. by Marian DelVecchio* 5½ x 8½, 192 pp, b/w illus., Quality PB, 978-1-59473-137-2 **$15.99**

A Walk with Four Spiritual Guides: Krishna, Buddha, Jesus, and Ramakrishna
by Andrew Harvey 5½ x 8½, 192 pp, b/w photos & illus., Quality PB, 978-1-59473-138-9 **$15.99**

The Workplace and Spirituality: New Perspectives on Research and Practice
Edited by Dr. Joan Marques, Dr. Satinder Dhiman and Dr. Richard King
6 x 9, 256 pp, HC, 978-1-59473-260-7 **$29.99**

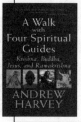

Spiritual Practice

Laugh Your Way to Grace: Reclaiming the Spiritual Power of Humor
by Rev. Susan Sparks A powerful, humorous case for laughter as a spiritual, healing path. 6 x 9, 176 pp, Quality PB, 978-1-59473-280-5 **$16.99**

Haiku—The Sacred Art: A Spiritual Practice in Three Lines
by Margaret D. McGee Introduces haiku as a simple and effective way of tapping into the sacred moments that permeate everyday living.
5½ x 8½, 192 pp, Quality PB, 978-1-59473-269-0 **$16.99**

Dance—The Sacred Art: The Joy of Movement as a Spiritual Practice
by Cynthia Winton-Henry Invites all of us, regardless of experience, into the possibility of dance/movement as a spiritual practice.
5½ x 8½, 224 pp, Quality PB, 978-1-59473-268-3 **$16.99**

Spiritual Adventures in the Snow: Skiing & Snowboarding as Renewal for Your Soul *by Dr. Marcia McFee and Rev. Karen Foster; Foreword by Paul Arthur*
Explores snow sports as tangible experiences of the spiritual essence of our bodies and the earth. 5½ x 8½, 208 pp, Quality PB, 978-1-59473-270-6 **$16.99**

Divining the Body: Reclaim the Holiness of Your Physical Self *by Jan Phillips*
8 x 8, 256 pp, Quality PB, 978-1-59473-080-1 **$16.99**

Everyday Herbs in Spiritual Life: A Guide to Many Practices
by Michael J. Caduto; Foreword by Rosemary Gladstar
7 x 9, 208 pp, 20+ b/w illus., Quality PB, 978-1-59473-174-7 **$16.99**

The Gospel of Thomas: A Guidebook for Spiritual Practice
by Ron Miller; Translations by Stevan Davies 6 x 9, 160 pp, Quality PB, 978-1-59473-047-4 **$14.99**

Hospitality—The Sacred Art: Discovering the Hidden Spiritual Power of
Invitation and Welcome *by Rev. Nanette Sawyer; Foreword by Rev. Dirk Ficca*
5½ x 8½, 208 pp, Quality PB, 978-1-59473-228-7 **$16.99**

Labyrinths from the Outside In: Walking to Spiritual Insight—A Beginner's
Guide *by Donna Schaper and Carole Ann Camp*
6 x 9, 208 pp, b/w illus. and photos, Quality PB, 978-1-893361-18-8 **$16.95**

Practicing the Sacred Art of Listening: A Guide to Enrich Your Relationships and
Kindle Your Spiritual Life *by Kay Lindahl* 8 x 8, 176 pp, Quality PB, 978-1-893361-85-0 **$16.95**

Recovery—The Sacred Art: The Twelve Steps as Spiritual Practice *by Rami Shapiro;
Foreword by Joan Borysenko, PhD* 5½ x 8½, 240 pp, Quality PB, 978-1-59473-259-1 **$16.99**

Running—The Sacred Art: Preparing to Practice *by Dr. Warren A. Kay; Foreword by
Kristin Armstrong* 5½ x 8½, 160 pp, Quality PB, 978-1-59473-227-0 **$16.99**

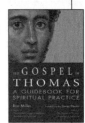

The Sacred Art of Bowing: Preparing to Practice
by Andi Young 5½ x 8½, 128 pp, b/w illus., Quality PB, 978-1-893361-82-9 **$14.95**

The Sacred Art of Chant: Preparing to Practice
by Ana Hernández 5½ x 8½, 192 pp, Quality PB, 978-1-59473-036-8 **$15.99**

The Sacred Art of Fasting: Preparing to Practice
by Thomas Ryan, CSP 5½ x 8½, 192 pp, Quality PB, 978-1-59473-078-8 **$15.99**

The Sacred Art of Forgiveness: Forgiving Ourselves and Others through God's Grace
by Marcia Ford 8 x 8, 176 pp, Quality PB, 978-1-59473-175-4 **$16.99**

The Sacred Art of Listening: Forty Reflections for Cultivating a Spiritual Practice
by Kay Lindahl; Illus. by Amy Schnapper 8 x 8, 160 pp, b/w illus., Quality PB, 978-1-893361-44-7 **$16.99**

The Sacred Art of Lovingkindness: Preparing to Practice
by Rabbi Rami Shapiro; Foreword by Marcia Ford 5½ x 8½, 176 pp, Quality PB, 978-1-59473-151-8 **$16.99**

Sacred Attention: A Spiritual Practice for Finding God in the Moment
by Margaret D. McGee 6 x 9, 144 pp, Quality PB, 978-1-59473-291-1 **$16.99**

Sacred Speech: A Practical Guide for Keeping Spirit in Your Speech
by Rev. Donna Schaper 6 x 9, 176 pp, Quality PB, 978-1-59473-068-9 **$15.99**
HC, 978-1-893361-74-4 **$21.95**

Soul Fire: Accessing Your Creativity
by Thomas Ryan, CSP 6 x 9, 160 pp, Quality PB, 978-1-59473-243-0 **$16.99**

Thanking & Blessing—The Sacred Art: Spiritual Vitality through Gratefulness
by Jay Marshall, PhD; Foreword by Philip Gulley 5½ x 8½, 176 pp, Quality PB, 978-1-59473-231-7 **$16.99**

Women's Interest

New Feminist Christianity: Many Voices, Many Views
Edited by Mary E. Hunt and Diann L. Neu
Insights from ministers and theologians, activists and leaders, artists and liturgists who are shaping the future. Taken together, their voices offer a starting point for building new models of religious life and worship.
6 x 9, 384 pp, HC, 978-1-59473-285-0 **$24.99**

New Jewish Feminism: Probing the Past, Forging the Future
Edited by Rabbi Elyse Goldstein; Foreword by Anita Diamant
Looks at the growth and accomplishments of Jewish feminism and what they mean for Jewish women today and tomorrow. Features the voices of women from every area of Jewish life, addressing the important issues that concern Jewish women.
6 x 9, 480 pp, HC, 978-1-58023-359-0 **$24.99***

Dance—The Sacred Art: The Joy of Movement as a Spiritual Practice
by Cynthia Winton-Henry 5½ x 8½, 224 pp, Quality PB, 978-1-59473-268-3 **$16.99**

Daughters of the Desert: Stories of Remarkable Women from Christian, Jewish and Muslim Traditions
by Claire Rudolf Murphy, Meghan Nuttall Sayres, Mary Cronk Farrell, Sarah Conover and Betsy Wharton
5½ x 8½, 192 pp, Illus., Quality PB, 978-1-59473-106-8 **$14.99** Inc. reader's discussion guide
HC, 978-1-893361-72-0 **$19.95**

The Divine Feminine in Biblical Wisdom Literature
Selections Annotated & Explained
Translation & Annotation by Rabbi Rami Shapiro; Foreword by Rev. Cynthia Bourgeault, PhD
5½ x 8½, 240 pp, Quality PB, 978-1-59473-109-9 **$16.99**

Divining the Body: Reclaim the Holiness of Your Physical Self
by Jan Phillips 8 x 8, 256 pp, Quality PB, 978-1-59473-080-1 **$16.99**

Honoring Motherhood: Prayers, Ceremonies & Blessings
Edited and with Introductions by Lynn L. Caruso 5 x 7¼, 272 pp, HC, 978-1-59473-239-3 **$19.99**

ReVisions: Seeing Torah through a Feminist Lens
by Rabbi Elyse Goldstein 5½ x 8½, 224 pp, Quality PB, 978-1-58023-117-6 **$16.95***

The Triumph of Eve & Other Subversive Bible Tales
by Matt Biers-Ariel 5½ x 8½, 192 pp, Quality PB, 978-1-59473-176-1 **$14.99**

Also available: **The Triumph of Eve Teacher's Guide**
8½ x 11, 44 pp, PB, 978-1-59473-152-5 **$8.99**

White Fire: A Portrait of Women Spiritual Leaders in America
by Malka Drucker; Photos by Gay Block 7 x 10, 320 pp, b/w photos, HC, 978-1-893361-64-5 **$24.95**

Woman Spirit Awakening in Nature
Growing Into the Fullness of Who You Are
by Nancy Barrett Chickerneo, PhD; Foreword by Eileen Fisher
8 x 8, 224 pp, b/w illus., Quality PB, 978-1-59473-250-8 **$16.99**

Women of Color Pray: Voices of Strength, Faith, Healing, Hope and Courage
Edited and with Introductions by Christal M. Jackson
5 x 7¼, 208 pp, Quality PB, 978-1-59473-077-1 **$15.99**

Women Pray: Voices through the Ages, from Many Faiths, Cultures and Traditions
Edited and with Introductions by Monica Furlong
5 x 7¼, 256 pp, Quality PB, 978-1-59473-071-9 **$15.99**

The Women's Haftarah Commentary: New Insights from Women Rabbis on the 54 Weekly Haftarah Portions, the 5 Megillot & Special Shabbatot *Edited by Rabbi Elyse Goldstein*
6 x 9, 560 pp, Quality PB, 978-1-58023-371-2 **$19.99***

The Women's Torah Commentary: New Insights from Women Rabbis on the 54 Weekly Torah Portions *Edited by Rabbi Elyse Goldstein*
6 x 9, 496 pp, Quality PB, 978-1-58023-370-5 **$19.99**; HC, 978-1-58023-076-6 **$34.95***

* A book from Jewish Lights, SkyLight Paths' sister imprint

Prayer / Meditation

Sacred Attention: A Spiritual Practice for Finding God in the Moment
by Margaret D. McGee
Framed on the Christian liturgical year, this inspiring guide explores ways to develop a practice of attention as a means of talking—and listening—to God.
6 x 9, 144 pp, Quality PB, 978-1-59473-291-1 **$16.99**

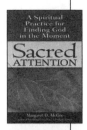

Women Pray: Voices through the Ages, from Many Faiths, Cultures and Traditions
Edited and with Introductions by Monica Furlong
5 x 7¼, 256 pp, Quality PB, 978-1-59473-071-9 **$15.99**

Women of Color Pray: Voices of Strength, Faith, Healing, Hope and Courage
Edited and with Introductions by Christal M. Jackson
Through these prayers, poetry, lyrics, meditations and affirmations, you will share in the strong and undeniable connection women of color share with God.
5 x 7¼, 208 pp, Quality PB, 978-1-59473-077-1 **$15.99**

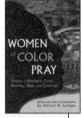

Secrets of Prayer: A Multifaith Guide to Creating Personal Prayer in
Your Life   *by Nancy Corcoran, CSJ*
This compelling, multifaith guidebook offers you companionship and encouragement on the journey to a healthy prayer life.   6 x 9, 160 pp, Quality PB, 978-1-59473-215-7 **$16.99**

Prayers to an Evolutionary God
by William Cleary; Afterword by Diarmuid O'Murchu
Inspired by the spiritual and scientific teachings of Diarmuid O'Murchu and Teilhard de Chardin, reveals that religion and science can be combined to create an expanding view of the universe—an evolutionary faith.
6 x 9, 208 pp, HC, 978-1-59473-006-1 **$21.99**

The Art of Public Prayer, 2nd Edition: Not for Clergy Only
by Lawrence A. Hoffman, PhD   6 x 9, 288 pp, Quality PB, 978-1-893361-06-5 **$19.99**

A Heart of Stillness: A Complete Guide to Learning the Art of Meditation
by David A. Cooper   5½ x 8½, 272 pp, Quality PB, 978-1-893361-03-4 **$18.99**

Meditation without Gurus: A Guide to the Heart of Practice
by Clark Strand   5½ x 8½, 192 pp, Quality PB, 978-1-893361-93-5 **$16.95**

Praying with Our Hands: 21 Practices of Embodied Prayer from the World's
Spiritual Traditions   *by Jon M. Sweeney; Photos by Jennifer J. Wilson; Foreword by Mother Tessa
Bielecki; Afterword by Taitetsu Unno, PhD*
8 x 8, 96 pp, 22 duotone photos, Quality PB, 978-1-893361-16-4 **$16.95**

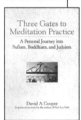

Three Gates to Meditation Practice: A Personal Journey into Sufism, Buddhism,
and Judaism   *by David A. Cooper*   5½ x 8½, 240 pp, Quality PB, 978-1-893361-22-5 **$16.95**

Prayer / M. Basil Pennington, OCSO

Finding Grace at the Center, 3rd Edition: The Beginning of
Centering Prayer   *with Thomas Keating, OCSO, and Thomas E. Clarke, SJ; Foreword by Rev. Cynthia
Bourgeault, PhD*   A practical guide to a simple and beautiful form of meditative prayer.   5 x 7¼, 128 pp, Quality PB, 978-1-59473-182-2 **$12.99**

The Monks of Mount Athos: A Western Monk's Extraordinary
Spiritual Journey on Eastern Holy Ground   *Foreword by Archimandrite Dionysios*
Explores the landscape, monastic communities and food of Athos.
6 x 9, 352 pp, Quality PB, 978-1-893361-78-2 **$18.95**

Psalms: A Spiritual Commentary   *Illus. by Phillip Ratner*
Reflections on some of the most beloved passages from the Bible's most widely read book.   6 x 9, 176 pp, 24 full-page b/w illus., Quality PB, 978-1-59473-234-8 **$16.99**

The Song of Songs: A Spiritual Commentary   *Illus. by Phillip Ratner*
Explore the Bible's most challenging mystical text.
6 x 9, 160 pp, 14 full-page b/w illus., Quality PB, 978-1-59473-235-5 **$16.99**
HC, 978-1-59473-004-7 **$19.99**

About SKYLIGHT PATHS Publishing

SkyLight Paths Publishing is creating a place where people of different spiritual traditions come together for challenge and inspiration, a place where we can help each other understand the mystery that lies at the heart of our existence.

Through spirituality, our religious beliefs are increasingly becoming a part of our lives—rather than *apart* from our lives. While many of us may be more interested than ever in spiritual growth, we may be less firmly planted in traditional religion. Yet, we do want to deepen our relationship to the sacred, to learn from our own as well as from other faith traditions, and to practice in new ways.

SkyLight Paths sees both believers and seekers as a community that increasingly transcends traditional boundaries of religion and denomination—people wanting to learn from each other, *walking together, finding the way.*

For your information and convenience, at the back of this book we have provided a list of other SkyLight Paths books you might find interesting and useful. They cover the following subjects:

Buddhism / Zen	Global Spiritual	Monasticism
Catholicism	Perspectives	Mysticism
Children's Books	Gnosticism	Poetry
Christianity	Hinduism /	Prayer
Comparative	Vedanta	Religious Etiquette
Religion	Inspiration	Retirement
Current Events	Islam / Sufism	Spiritual Biography
Earth-Based	Judaism	Spiritual Direction
Spirituality	Kabbalah	Spirituality
Enneagram	Meditation	Women's Interest
	Midrash Fiction	Worship